A Cynical Guide to Corporate Jobs & Office Politics

Strategies for Surviving and Thriving in the Working World

RICK LAZARUS

"Feeling confronted with the absurdity of life may sometimes nurture a personal satisfaction for those who like to set a paramount task or to create a compassionate mission.

In so doing, the seal of absurdity becomes less unbearable, while it confers them a 'Sisyphus' status that transmutes them into heroes of human resilience."

("Sisyphus on the Hill"- Erik Pevernagie)

Content

3. The Art of Concealment

4. Projecting the Right Image

5. The Daily Grind

6. Realpolitik

Preface

Welcome dear readers to the world of unadulterated cynicism. This book does not encourage negativity or pessimistic thoughts, but rather a belief that people are motivated purely by self-interest (i.e. people are selfish bastards by default), and therefore recommends a growth mind-set which revolves around such notion of the human condition.

If you agree with me, you're in good company for a healthy dose of candid and forthcoming advice on corporations, work life and office politics, written with cynical insights and gumption. There are no feel-good messages and generic "professional platitudes", but only raw, ugly truths. Not many self-help books dare to go down this path, because the publishers may not like it. Since this book is self-published, I have the liberty to hit close to home, warts and all.

This book is written for the employees, the job-hunters, the men in the street and basically anybody interested to know what corporations and office politics are like, and how to handle them. Most of you readers are also likely disgruntled, because let's face it, that's probably the main reason why you read the book.

Most people would agree that working for other people sucks. But we've got to acknowledge that it is the only source of income for most people. Unless there are other ways to secure sustainable sources of income, there is nothing much anybody can do except to go through it and put up with it. This book will serve to make the process better and rewarding.

This book is exactly dealing with things which the average employees are fed up about; the slimy and evil corporations, the extent of human vileness therein, the bitchy politics, and ways to get around and thrive in a slavish obligation known as employment. These insights are a culmination from my years of experiences with the working world, a rags to riches life of constant observations and strategies.

I began at a lower strata than the men in the street, holding down several jobs and barely making ends meet. Being disenfranchised in many ways during my formative years, I was desperate to improve my situations.

I was sick, poor, and could not hold up my head.

One of the place I used to work in when I was a teenager was at this dingy restaurant as a dishwasher. Confined in the scullery at the back of the restaurant kitchen, I had to wash the cutlery and clean the shit left behind by everyone. Then a guy who just joined was promoted to become the supervisor in charge of all the dishwashers and kitchen hands. He had no prior relation to the restaurant owner and wasn't the most hardworking person, but he was certainly good with words.

There seemed to be some kind of epiphany which struck me when that guy became the supervisor; I came to realize that in order to get to a better position in job, it is not about how hard you work, but rather how you act and behave. I washed the dishes hard and was going nowhere but paid pittance.

Throughout my different odd jobs, having to also constantly deal with bullies and nasty people, I got interested in reading human cues and examining the human condition, analyzing motivations and formulating strategies to deal with people. Life's struggles seem to be about "dealing with people".

After leaving the odd jobs, and finishing so called education, I joined the corporate worlds. By then I was already armed with many insights and skills on "dealing with people". I fine tuned those lessons I had in my formative years and began a very long journey of strategic living. The people in the corporate worlds were obviously another breed from those in my odd job days: much more complex, devious and dangerous. I constantly observed those monstrosities and situations, and revised my strategies in the process. The notion of "dealing with people" was added another dimension: the key to survival pointed to "adaptability" which I had learnt.

I saw many of my former colleagues who knew how to talk and behave, and still got side lined because they lacked that adaptability and cleverness to get into the winning side. I saw how the superstars in the corporate world fell from grace, and black sheep surprising everyone in the industry. The winners take it all, the losers take the fall. Carefully I tread and I began my long journey from a lowly office staff to be in the ranks of senior executive and directorship. Those accolades and successes benchmarked me towards other goals in life, primarily: Financial Freedom. But coming from a humble background, I know that I can only get to my primary goal by joining the rat race and climbing towards the heights of corporate ladder. In case the reader hasn't realize, I hate employment, the corporation and the rat race and I used to work because I had no choice. But it was an inevitable journey nonetheless, a necessary evil and rite of passage.

The average reader probably felt the same way; you probably have no choice and have to stick to a job. In that case, then try to make the journey smoother, less painful and more rewarding. In this book, I am sharing the insights and strategies which have allowed me to survive and thrive well in my career. This book will inform and empower you in the corporate world and its inherently political nature.

A strong impetus for writing the book is also due to the fact that many self-help books are not effective. It is no surprise that many of these books are written by the baby boomers (people born between 1944-1964) with outdated formula for success. I grew up reading their books and had made several mistakes by following their advice. I had better results sticking with my own strategies. What could be so fundamentally wrong? It is also addressed in this book.

Rick Lazarus 2019 (*Sic itur ad astra*)

1. The Red Pill

The "red pill" brings a life of harsh knowledge, desperate freedom and the brutal truths of reality.

We are taught from young to have a good education, to work hard for our living, get married, have kids and then retire comfortably. When kids get out of college and find a job, that is frequently celebrated by family and friends, although in reality, it marks the embarkation into one of the hardest phase of life.

Working adults are frequently beaten down by the harsh realities of working life. Many of them who had ideals and aspirations, some of which were formed during the days of exuberant youth, saw those dreams crushed when they cannot match up to the reality- which is one of those major contributing factors to depression in the modern society. They struggled with work, had their plans hijacked by the people they met in the workplace, and felt like going nowhere in their career.

I know a lot of people who face problems at work, but can't find ways to improve the situation. They may not have the insight to know exactly what is wrong, and therefore every time they can only react to the problems, without treating at the roots of the problems, and may be doomed to repeat them again. In better times, it is prudent to first understand why things are the way they are; why jobs exist, why do one get into employment, why the sufferings; before zooming into the details of the problems.

Insights are based on common sense, but are not common because the masses are veiled in a cloak of distraction, deceit and dissonance, conceived from wrongful notions either passed down by those who didn't know better or pulled wool over eyes by deliberation of power agents.

In order to gain insights, one has to first take a step back, examine the bigger picture for what it is, and then take the right step forward towards precision, and correct action. I am making things simpler by helping to unveil the cloak, laying out the road map in the process, and it begins by first opening up the readers to the reality of problems in the working world at the macro level; it may not seem apparent as immediate to the problems that the readers may be facing right now, but these are the roots of many problems associated with the working world and even the ills of our modern society.

After the reader consumes the Red Pill, the rest of the journey becomes lucid.

The journey begins here.

The Great Miseducation

Let's begin by looking at the current state of the world, at a modern day problem which is pervasive these days- The Great Miseducation. Most of the working adults today are currently constituted of children of baby boomers (baby boomers are born between 1944-1964).

They are the generation brought up by the education and ethos that were effectively inculcated by their parents with mind-set from post-war periods, and which have become sadly impractical and outdated in contemporary times.

One example of this miseducation is with work ethics: they taught that education, conformity and hard work will eventually pay off; but when we start to look around us, we realize these are fallacious (we have seen how much of it didn't eventually work out), especially when the world transits into the new millennia. There is nothing wrong with education, conformity and hard work, indeed they are definitely valuable, but if they are taken at face value, they do not necessarily guarantee success. They need to be updated.

Hard work needs to be applied selectively. Hard work expends energy, and one should focus on the right areas to work on, in the most expedient way, with the greatest amount of ROI (return of investment). The labor economy of the past is rapidly replaced by knowledge economy at an unprecedented scale; we see factory operations getting automated, replacing line operators with robots; we see many agencies and brick and mortar shops shutting down, with the advent of internet, online quoting and online shopping; we see the power of social media, spelling certain doom for legacy media and newspapers.

The main currency sought in this era is- Time. In the old economy, and still in certain parts of the third world, labor is cheap because time is cheap; the average laborer can toil away at work for a long time, at a low wage and high cost (energy). The new economy values that the same work can be performed at shorter time, and at a lower cost. With the same amount of time used, more work can be done, and therefore the person is paid higher wages. The key to better expediency and higher ROI lies in knowledge and information. To know better on how to work better, to have access to information that can add on the knowledge- they can drive innovations, and therefore expediency.

Conformity needs to be observed appropriately. The baby boomers are a generation who fully epitomize the label 'sheeples'. Understandably, the post-war drive towards nation building is one laden with the most amount of propaganda, with systematic brainwashing that conditions an average person into obedience (or subservience) in preparation for the rapidly expanding industries; to obey the rules, follow the laws, toe the line, do the right things, think the right way, foster and uphold the right values, respect authority, and fear unemployment. Yet I want to qualify that it is always prudent to conform at the workplace, it is a quality that is encouraged in the book; but I want the readers to understand the difference between conformity in appearance vs conformity in the heart. Always act like you are conforming, but do not get it into the heart, because it will curb creativity and encourage herd mentality. In order to get ahead in the career game, one has to think differently from the masses.

Education needs to be holistic, and decentralized. Most of our education are still largely institutionalized, and in line with national schemes. Most baby boomers believe that schools provide sufficient education. They were taught that if someone studied hard at school and gets good results, he or she was therefore sufficiently educated and well primed for success at the career. And towards the '80s, they started to believe that the key to success required college degrees.

From the schools and from their TV sets, they were sold a dream, perhaps an American Dream whereby all they would ever need to do was to study hard, get a job, do well in the job, get married, have kids and afterwards they will surely have a house, a car, and a dog named Boo. The ultimate goals lie in retirement and 401K.

What they fail to understand is that the schools are insufficient to educate, because they only serve to improve certain skills and disciplines, and they are boot camps to condition the students to think in a certain one track mind, especially if they are government schools. A holistic education requires exposure, to as many different sources as possible, especially in the new knowledge economy.

The work ethics of the baby boomers is a tried and tested formula that worked well only for the baby boomers. Unfortunately, this model is still passed down as a legacy to our generation, and are increasingly ineffective and outdated for our time, despite the evident transition from the labor to the knowledge economy.

It doesn't help at all that many of the self-help books on jobs and careers we see in the market are largely written by the same people, the baby boomers.

Perspectives on Employment

Why do you have to work? It is not the most pleasant thing to do, especially when you do not enjoy your work. Yet you are obliged to follow through the same routine every workday.

Why are you afraid of unemployment?

Does losing your job not equate to gaining freedom to do what you always wanted to do?

The main reason obviously lies with the reality that working for a job brings in income, and it is with this income that helps bring in the dough, to pay off the cost of living, to improve the quality of life, and perhaps, to build the resources for endeavor and other aspirations. Most people primarily get incomes from jobs, and this is what keeps the job market going. In order to get perspectives on the job market, we have to first define the terms.

Work is defined as activity involving mental or physical effort done in order to achieve a purpose or result. It does not necessarily means that it involves job in employment. You can work in the gardens for your own pleasure. You can work freelance and get paid without having to report to a boss. But in this context, work is performed at jobs, which involves employment.

Income is defined as money received, especially on a regular basis, for work or through investments. It does not has to only come from a job, paid by a company, although it is the most common way most people get income. Income can also come in through many forms from active sources: offering a service, day trading; and passive sources: dividends, royalties.

Job is defined as paid position of regular employment. Usually a job require certain amount of work hours, and a certain amount of skill set. Most jobs are performed in the office, and the employee is managed through a supervisor. It is possible to also get freelance job, ad hoc job without formal employment settings.

Employment is the state of having paid job. It usually begins with a mutually consented contract between the employer and the employee, stating the terms and conditions, the job descriptions, and the payment amount. It is an obligation for the employee to observe and undertake.

Jobs are created by companies, and driven by industries which essentially created the job market (or employment market). Employment rates are often important factors influencing economic growth and GDPs, and often reflect the overall status of the economy. Employment at a deeper level however bears the burden of age-old problems, which begins with debt.

1. **Debt**- The whole world is sinking deeper into debt burden because they are created excessively and also do not really fall, but passed around different sectors

and countries, where monetary policies are inadequate to stimulate global demand, rather than to redistribute it.

Debt has been around for ages since prehistory of mankind (examples: indentured servitude to debt owners- serfdom). Human beings even tend to subconsciously couch the language of love with debt in transactional terms (examples: I owe my parents a favor; I hope Jesus can redeem my sins).

2. **Corporation**- The really big and powerful ones are the current day debt owners along with its bankster brethren. It is a business entity that is legally separate from its owners, whereby the latter are the shareholders, with percentage ownership by corporate stocks or shares.

The aim of the corporation primarily is to make money, to pay the shareholders. They can become global (Multi-National Corporations-MNCs) and get so big that they monopolize the market.

The conglomerate of some of the biggest corporations (and banks) arguably have more power than many states. At the negative side, the entity seemingly takes on a characteristic on its own, bent on higher profit margins, exploitation and having general disregard for social responsibilities. The world is now evidently run by oligarchs, whereby state affairs are frequently tied in, or intervened by these powerful corporations.

3. **Servitude**- The average person is born to serve debt, for the corporate masters, even when the person is not directly working for any corporations (or has a clean credit score). Most people are obliged to work (labor is used broadly here, and even though we are in the knowledge economy, there is still labor performed).

We work in jobs in exchange for wages to sustain our living. We build careers out of jobs, as a necessary step to advance our worth and purpose in society, as well as for our personal satisfaction. While we seem to be able to make choices when it comes to jobs, our contribution to the wage slavery system is largely obligatory, unless we have enough resources to say good riddance to the employers.

The work tie is a reminder of this servitude, a symbol of slavery, resembling the noose tied around the neck of the slave; but instead of getting tightened by the slavemasters, the average person voluntarily tightens it around their neck.

4. **Globalization**- The world is increasingly getting smaller and more interconnected. It was unimaginable even 30 years ago for a Congolese to interact with a Chinese, but this is happening all over the world right now, thanks to technological advances, which bridges gap and saves time. MNCs are getting into more regions, pushing their products into more markets, creating global cultural narratives, with a character that

challenges traditional status quo (conservatism, existing communities).

5. **The New Economy**- Because of globalization, many hard labors (or more dangerous/unpleasant works) are outsourced to poorer nations or countries with cheaper labor costs. In more developed nations, the knowledge economy is placed at priority over the labor economy, where expediency is more valued.

   Expediency drives innovation, which in turn drives economy; technology sprouted, money is made faster, and pace of life increases. The new economy also created new attitude, especially evident from the millennial generation, whereby there is a surfeit of information, instant gratification, and more individualistic yet socially involved engagements.

The advent of the new economy actually has an effect on employment; less workers are needed in frontend processes in developed nations, like procurement of raw material, manufacturing, production, as they are largely outsourced to developing nations or automated, and even traditional agency and brick and mortar businesses are replaced by e-commerce.

Skills and knowledge can be obsolete at an extreme rate, especially when it concerns technology.

Every employee faces the daunting prospect of unemployment. It may come a time when certain professions are no longer valued, and the servitude is not even needed anymore, if the corporations find other means to profiteering. But before that happens to any of the readers, employment is still a painful obligation in most people's life.

Corporate Slavery

In 1865, the 13th amendment abolished slavery in the United States and provides that "Neither slavery nor involuntary servitude, except as a punishment for crime whereof the party shall have been duly convicted, shall exist within the United States, or any place subject to their jurisdiction." In the rest of the world, it was not until 2007 that slavery was criminalized in one of the last stronghold of serfdom, Mauritania. Yet some form of slavery still persisted, and the most apparent one is: Corporate Slavery.

Though reforms and abolitionism, we would have gathered that mankind has transcended towards higher human standards, compassion and enlightenment. However, we are never truly free from the yoke of slavery.

Corporate cultures are all encompassing in contemporary times, stretching its oligarchical tentacles throughout the modern world for hegemony and profiteering. Everybody from the states level down to the individuals could not shake off these all pervasive effects of the power of corporations and its ruthless machinery for margins.

Unless you are born with a silver spoon, there is a likelihood that you, along with most of humanity is still enslaved by corporations. The machinery is so deeply entrenched in modern day society that you inadvertently contribute your labor and time to benefit the cogs and wheels of this system, enriching it either directly or indirectly. Most people would have worked as employees in their adulthood.

The small business enterprise employers may be far from the gargantuan Multi-National Corporations (MNCs), but they are still all part of this corporate system as long as they pay taxes to the government, transact in currencies and incur costs through expenses, because most of these money will eventually go back to the big corporate conglomerates.

If you are reading this book, there is a good chance that you are still obliged to have a job (and face the boss and the office). There is not much of a choice for most of the common folks, because without work, there will be disruption of income, making it difficult to put bread on the table- to sustain life and its costs of living.

All wage employees are slaves to the machine, starting from the CEO and the management as Slavemasters (actually more appropriate to call them Master Slaves) down to the menial labor drones who are the majority; never mind that annoying acquaintance of yours with the fanciful title and the penthouse- he is also a corporate slave if he works for a job. Once we acknowledge this sad fact of life, we will be more resolved, though not resigning ourselves to fate, but to work our way towards one possible way of freedom from this corporate slavery.

Job is a Necessary Evil

The most likely freedom anyone can try to attempt is financial freedom; which can enable one with the choice of not having to have a job (and face the boss and the office), and effectively getting out of the rat race.

Financial freedom means having steady amount of money to be not dependent on slave income or say good riddance to employers. However, financial freedom is not easily attained unless one has the necessary acumen, opportunity and resources. Barring that, it is highly probable that one of the sole avenue for income for most is through having a job.

Job= Corporate Slavery= Evil, but a necessary one.

Job sucks. Nobody fancies toiling in a roomful of people they don't like, to do the things they don't necessarily enjoy, and to put up with the nonsense from the superiors. But it may surprisingly be the ticket out of corporate slavery, as ironic as it sounds.

A job is defined as a paid position of regular employment-corporate slavery regardless of whether it is a relaxing or unpleasant one. Working for jobs unfortunately is a mean to an end, but not an end to itself. Most of us have to suck it up and have jobs and therefore we are definitely corporate slaves at some point in our life. Yet this is a necessary evil for the indigent.

Because jobs provide: acumen, experience with people/market, problem solving skills, fulfilment of societal expectations, exposure to opportunities and most importantly salary. These are things useful for us to plan for entrepreneurship and/or financial freedom if you want them. Otherwise they are good for the resume and career.

The small amount of freedom we can exercise when it comes to job is choice. You have a choice of jobs. And usually the types of job choices are tied to certain preferences or inclinations. If the wrong choices are made, or if by misfortune one is stuck in job types that do not reflect the preferences and inclinations, then one might have to ponder and attempt to revisit such choices. Having made good choices of jobs are usually helpful to build up a career.

Career is viewed quite differently from a job, with its own definition- an occupation undertaken for a significant period of a person's life and with opportunities for progress. Career, can be a series of jobs or endeavors which build up a characteristic and form a narrative of a person's place and worth in the world. Granted that career may not necessarily lead to financial freedom, it certainly should at least lead to certain self actualization, personal satisfaction and more comfortable living, if done well.

Entrepreneurship is a hot topic in contemporary times, as more and more people are attempting such endeavor, partly for personal interest and largely to break out of the corporate slave cycle. Most people can start a business if they want to, but the endeavor may not be profitable or sustainable. Many young people these days are taking the plunge into entrepreneurship the moment they get out of college and most of them get themselves burnt and wrecked in the process because they lack the necessary experiences, capital and acumen to get their businesses to work. If they are more prudent, they will go through a proper part of the rites of initiation- to have a job to get experience.

Corporate slavery it is, but jobs expose us to the market, allowing us to have good understanding of society, human nature and the complex interpersonal dynamics between people, teaching us valuable lessons and to challenge us with real life problems that we can creatively apply our critical thinking, problem solving and risk management skills, making us more experienced, resilient and increasing our acumen and opportunities identification in the process, and I cannot reiterate enough- giving us the money we need.

When we go through jobs and achieve moderate amount of successes, it can form a rather pleasing narrative of our career, equip us with the knowledge, capital and acumen to attempt entrepreneurship, and most importantly prepare us with a good amount of skill sets and opportunity to achieve financial freedom, and thereafter to break out of the slave cycle, depending on whether one is prepared to or inclined to, or not of course. It is ironic- while corporate slavery is evil, one of the way to get out of it is to actually go through it first.

But before that happens, one has to suck it up, obviously toiling along as a slave to the grind, in all misery- blood, sweat and tears, and one day, one may find oneself rising to the ranks of slave masters, before attempting the leap of calculated faith towards liberation.

Right now, the next best thing the wage workers can do is to see how one can fare successfully in jobs, mitigating the nasties and augmenting the benefits- which is what this book is all about.

What the Companies Really Care About

Every companies that get to a decent size often have their own set of "Core Values", especially once they have enough budget to publish those little sets of platitudes on what they stand for. These statements are usually produced to make themselves look professional and to attract customers and investors alike; while the secondary intent (usually misconceived by many as the primary intent) is to have these values reinforced by the Human Resources onto its employees. "Core Values" usually revolve around positive sounding terms/phrases, like 'Teamwork', 'Integrity', etc made in such a fanciful manner to mean very simple hidden messages: absolute loyalty and dedicated slavery to the company.

Behind the façade of the optimistic phrases in "core values", every company (including those that did not put out "core value" statements) are generally concerned by these Real Values, ranked in priority:

1. **Positive Numbers**- This equals profit, good cashflow, more money for business growth or simply to look good on annual report for the investors. Numbers are crucial to the life and death of the company and 'Negative Numbers' are disliked. All employees have a set of

'Numbers' labelled on their heads, balanced by 'contributions' vs 'costs'. The employer's hope is that having their employees will bring about direct or indirect contribution to 'Positive Numbers' to the organization. Direct contributors are usually the commercial employees like sales & marketing personnel, and their value is simply measured by the revenue they bring in. Indirect contributors are the other employees that will inadvertently help to bring about these numbers through other functions in the company, for example operations personnel to ensure that the company will see through a seamless process in having its product to customers or the project scientists and engineers coming up with new products which the company can then sell.

The employees are then constantly measured by the "costs" (in financial term, actually expenses incurred through salary and incentives/bonus payouts) and balanced with their 'contributions' to see if they bring about positive 'Numbers' over a period of time. If proven "costly" after balancing out, the person is deemed not of value and therefore very disposable. However, human beings are complex creatures, and sometimes these 'Numbers' value cannot be properly assessed, especially in a large organization with many complex layers. E.g. a weak performer favored by boss can stay for a long time, even promoted.

2. **Safety**- From the moment any business begins, it will face imminent threat from rivals. Sabotages and legal

suits are frequent affairs, so any smart business owners will engage legal advice for their documentation, even to have their own legal employee if they have enough money. Depending on the nature of the business: security, regulatory affairs, trade compliance, policy people are also employed to ensure that nothing goes wrong to threaten the business. Even accountants are deemed valuable enough to protect the company, should one day the finances are called to question.

However, an even greater kind of danger is of utmost concern to any organization; and that is sabotage from within. It can range from leaking out confidential or proprietary information, to hijacking the business operations. The companies are especially paranoid about perceived danger, real or imagined, coming from its own internal employees and will therefore monitor or even spy on its employees while hoping that they will be inculcated "Core Values" like 'Integrity'. Any misdemeanor will result in negative actions (firing, or worse legal action) against the employee, faster and more decisive than when the employees are not hitting the numbers.

3. **Good Image**- Almost every company that gets large or famous enough, will try to brand themselves as ambassadors for a greater social cause. They will claim their products can contribute to the welfare or betterment of humanity, and they will allocate one major day in the year for all their employees to

participate in charity work, usually with some level of media coverage or photo evidence, to show the world that they are the good guys. These are of course all pretence and hypocrisy at the highest zenith, since the ultimate objective of any business is to make money (often at the expense of society). Only in the 21st century can we find such awkward term like 'Social Enterprises' which of course is an oxymoron (or the founder is deluded enough to believe in this bullshit).

The practical purpose of engaging in social causes and charitable works, is to give the company a 'Good Image', which will logically lead to increased business (Positive Numbers contributor), as well as increased reputation (Safety net contributor). However, it also serves tax reliefs (Positive Numbers contributor). The company expects its employees to always uphold 'Good Image' by showing positive aspects of the company (via social media like Linkedin or Glassdoor), and will tend to value employees who believe (or pretend to believe) in their bullshit.

4. **Smooth Operations**- Efficiency and expediency are parts of the equation which measures the interplay of time and cost, the factor that will ultimately translate into 'Numbers' for the business. Every business owner like its employees to toe the line, to be able to commit all their time, and all their best into the job. Whenever they sense the employee is capable of performing a lot within a short time, they will gladly pile more work onto that employee. Every business also hope that its

operation will run smoothly without problem. If there are no problems in the business, workers will not even be hired in the first place, therefore the employee is expected to solve problems, and better still, not to give any problems.

When a worker creates trouble, can't participate well in the team, exhibits signs of discontent, or shows intention of quitting, the company will identify this employee as a problem and annoyance. They will recite the Core Values (e.g. Teamwork, Positive Attitude) on the employee and find ways to make the employee improve (on their own terms), although the reasons behind the discontent of the employees are generally down played, ignored or covered up, especially if it involves office politics. Even when things improve, it does not change the fact that the HR/company would have already planned contingency plans against this worker, usually not to his or her benefit.

The Office
A Secular Purgatory

It's 5am, AGAIN, in the morning on a weekday and what a terrible feeling it is. The low quality sleep was prematurely broken, disturbed by the utter dread of the apprehension to face another day at work... AGAIN- to be in the company with those co-workers you don't like to see, performing tasks you don't necessarily enjoy; while you are struggling to reboot half the body again, feeling unrested. Then comes the mad hours, the frustrating commute and eventually the place you dread to see: the office.

One may have heard from some of their peers about the luxury of working remotely from home; but even in modern times, it constitutes a minority in today's work environment- 95% of the employees are still required to be in the office; and on time.

The office is a secular purgatory, where souls eke out a living indefinitely for the hope of redemption. Many times, even a sliver of hope is lost. There are some who sought refuge in the office, especially when they have problems at home- this makes the office even more miserable due to the presence of such miserable souls. Purgatory can be a scarier place than Hell because it is a place where the suspense hangs in standstill and suffering seemingly lengthened by the uncertainty.

The office can greatly attrition the will for resistance, beating the average worker into neutered drone. You are allocated to a location somewhere within the four walls where you will likely be confined to a sedentary position with a personal computer and a cup, either in a communal prison cell, or in some cases solitary confinement; like Alcatraz or a mental asylum. Not absolute hell, but close; the office is also teeming with all manner of dangerous life-forms not unlike the Serengeti, some obviously dangerous, some deceptively nice. The problem is you can't get out of this confinement, and have to be in the company with these monsters.

Survivors learnt well to condition themselves and adapt to this arena, putting on the masks of reticence and learning the art of poker face, forming grand tactics and strategies in periods of thoughtfulness and staying resilient, alert and clever in the process. The first thing that needs to happen is to grapple with this reality and starts getting used to the office (even if dread sets in the moment one step into the vicinity) by trying to look at the bright side of things.

The office can be a great training ground to gain experience, build character and study people. No matter how hard the work is, there are frequent respite for zoning out and contemplation of grand ideas. If one has no time even for zoning out; then one should seriously consider leaving this job for the next. The point of having a job is to consolidate experiences, skillsets and resources for the next move; either up the career ladder, or towards enterprise/financial freedom. The very nature of routine (or regiment) of going to the office and sitting through 9 to 5 (it can vary) is a great way to instill discipline and perseverance.

The second thing that employees could do is learning to co-exist amongst the different life-forms, be it malevolent or meek. The valuable experience and advantage that the office workers have over those who either do not work in the office or has not yet/never have a history in employment is the exposure to all manner of human types and dynamics. One of the very important key to success in life is to have lessons on human nature.

Every successful business, art, entertainment, and endeavor understood very well the human aspects; from basal needs and desires, to motivation and behavior. If one of the above is your planned undertaking in the future, you should learn about human beings as much as possible during periods of employment, and what better way to learn these than from the office?

On Office Politics

Real work is actually not the hardest part of the job; it is the office politics that is the most soul crushing and energy draining. When we hear about people hating their jobs, having problems with work or resigning from a company, they almost have something to do with office politics.

Office politics can result in many umbrage, from getting ostracized in the office, to getting backstabbed. Office politics do not always necessarily have to involve groups; it can also be one on one or personal. And office politics are known to thrive in any office- as long as one is in the company of human beings, there is always politics; the only difference is whether there is some of it or lots of it.

The 'Toxic Office' is the one that is festering with an unhealthily high level of office politics and ill will, and its poisonous miasma is sometimes so potent that it causes bad health both physically and mentally, and it might take years for the individual to flush out of his or her systems.

Every employee who goes to the office has to come to terms with a sad slice of reality; that office politics exist, and it's very real, raw, rough and relentless. But when one comes to terms with it, it is usually much easier to deal with, just like how one has to eventually accept the fact that it is part of human nature.

Human beings are social apes by nature but a rather divisive lot. Speaking of apes, our nature is more akin to the genocidal Chimpanzees than the peace-loving hippies known as Bonobos.

The primary reasons for major world conflicts are always due to differences: gender, religion, race, class, ideology, moral, culture etc. On a smaller scale, divisions also manifest in almost every aspect of life, from sibling rivalry and squabbles to argument over whether cornflakes is better soft or crispy.

One of the key reasons behind division is due to hegemony. Everyone consciously or subconsciously like their own ideas or kinds better, prefer to be in the same group who thinks, looks or behaves like them, and not in favor of the 'others'. Even within Multi-National Corporations (MNCs), which often preach diversity, one can quite often find people of the same color clustering together in their own groups, away from the rest, when they finally get enough of 'cultural interactions'.

This book talks a great deal about office politics. Dealing with office politics cleverly is probably one of the most important factors for survival during employment. One may not be able to get out of office politics, but you can still get ahead, and on top of office politics; it starts first by having a good grasp of human nature. Because it is simply all just about humans.

And There is a Boss

The Boss is defined as a person who is in charge of the worker or the organization. He or she can be the proprietor of the company; or simply the supervisor on top of the employee, a waged employee like everyone else. He or she is the person who has the most profound effect on the employee because it seems like the working life largely revolve around this person; who has certain power to herald relief or misery, admiration or contempt; or in rare instances none of the above. In any case, the employee should have a clear understanding on the characteristics or motivations of this person, who happen to be in a higher place in the hierarchy of the Corporate Slavery construct:

1. **The Boss like everyone else is only a mere mortal.** He or she is equally as fallible, imperfect as the next person. He or she is driven by similar motivations: to enrich either himself or herself; or to keep afloat in the fiscal situation, to sustain either a duty or a life's work. He or she has the same problems like the next person, when it comes to basal needs, emotions, security, reputation, power.

2. **The Boss is there for a good reason**; either because he or she has proven his or her self worth, fortunate or lucky enough to be in this position, or have enough

resources to run this endeavor. In this hierarchy of Corporate Slavery construct, you are relegated to a position that is below The Boss, and therefore you are generally obliged to do his or her bidding.

3. **The Boss is dynamic**, not in a sense of attitude, but in a sense that he or she is equally influenced by the tides and ebb of time and circumstances, with no definite certainly in terms of position, stay, influence or power. He or she should not be viewed as a long term fixture, but rather someone who is as equally vulnerable to changes.

4. **The Boss generally has certain expectations of his or her subordinates**: a) do not bring unnecessary trouble or problem to him or her, b) can complete assigned tasks well and in time and thereafter make his or her job easier, and to bring benefits to him or her in terms of money, recognition, power and influence, c) that the subordinates are sufficiently well equipped to do the job without asking for too much help, yet not doing the job so well that he or she position is threatened. d) that the subordinate will always toe the line, remain as a subordinate, preferably his or her own, stay transigent and respect his or her authority.

5. **The Boss will not generally care too much for the well being of the subordinates**, unless the person brings him or her problems at work. The Boss is driven by the same selfish motivation as everyone else, especially if he or she is also a waged Corporate Slave.

6. **The Boss has strong direct and indirect effects on job satisfaction and career progression of the subordinate.** He or she is the usher of rewards and punishment, gatekeeper of progressions and demise, and influencer of power and reputation; regardless of whether he is a strong or weak boss. He or she, like everyone else in the company partakes in office politics, and these have consequences on the subordinates.

7. **The Boss can be either the boon or the bane of an employee's existence in the company.** Aside from the work to be done, there is a likely chance that he or her personality, behavior and attitude will manifest in the team that he or she is leading. There will definitely be subjective bias, preferences and pet peeves, different work styles, and other interpersonal dynamics that come into play. The employee is to be prepared to interact with a persona that is either agreeable or disagreeable with his or her own personality.

8. **The Boss should be treated as selfish and unpredictable by default**, no matter how nice this person is; because his or her priority should be clearly understood as selfish as the other employee- no one signs up for a job to make friends, but to get income, and hopefully to get more income, and more career progression. The wise employee should always come up with contingency plans in case there is a potential fallout.

The Boss is someone who you should constantly monitor; be it to side step conflict, assess his or her power and influence, getting a sense on his or her perception of yourself, and to see how they can influence your career development. This person is so important in anybody's career life that it can justify a book entirely dedicated to study. This book will sufficiently discuss all the necessary points.

Everyone is Dispensable

Everyone from the cleaning lady to the CEO are dispensable to the company. Every employee is but a statistic in the company. The truth hurts: most businesses (especially at a company level) generally doesn't care about you, as long as you don't create problems for them.

They will certainly enjoy and appreciate your loyalty (sometimes this may lead to a chuckle or two amongst the senior management); they will not value you as an individual once you transgress on their rules or don't serve their values, after which they will surely drop you like a hot potato without much concern or sentimentality.

The four main core values ("What the Companies Really Care About") which were mentioned before are selfish objectives for the well being of the business, and even if you perish or is obliterated from the face of the Earth, it is business as usual for them and you will most likely not be dearly missed, so don't take things too personally.

Knowing how cruel the nature of business is like, it is better for the wise employee to play along to its game, and deliver (or make it seem like one is able to deliver) those values that are important to the business. When at least three out of the four values which were mentioned, are evidently played out and conspicuous, the employee usually stands a chance to rise in rank, because every organization desperately desire and want such perfect slaves to sustain their money-making endeavors in posterity.

Do not be held sway by appreciations and promises of protection and benefits by the superiors for your loyalty or servitude; those are superfluous and insincere words to ensure that you don't give them problems by making the exit. Do not sell your soul to the company especially when there are no clear benefits in staying put there. Remember, your goal is to make a career out of yourself, and you should treat all your employers as stepping stones towards such aspiration.

No One Really Cares About You

When I said no one cares, it doesn't mean that people completely ignores you in the office. Quite the contrary, colleagues will watch and monitor one another all the time. The 'care' here is more about concern for well being.

The amount of apathy is strong especially in the workplace because employees sign up for work not to make friends or to find love (although those things do happen sometimes at the workplace); the very purpose of having a job is to get by life with salary to bring in the dough.

By default, you should treat everyone in your office as selfish bastards who only care for their own well being and survival in the company; no matter how nice, supportive and friendly they seem to be, because when shit hits the fan, it is more likely that none of them will go all out to help you, especially when it concerns you falling out with someone powerful and influential in the office, and/or your departure from the organization.

Everyone in the office are merely just playing out their roles, and they do not really care about you unless you have something to benefit them, or you might have developed few meaningful relationships with some of them. The 'buddy' who almost seems willing to fight tooth and nail for you when both of you are in the same department may turn cold and heartless when you are leaving the organization. When bad things happen to you, the concerned looks and supportive gestures from most of your co-workers in the office are merely acted out to make them seem more human and 'professional' (the empathetic employee quality); the Human Resources department has certain protocol to act out such roles with great finesse.

Since that is generally the case, you should not expect too much from your colleagues, especially when it concerns serious problems, because they are merely your colleagues, and not someone who genuinely matters.

Trust No One But Yourself

Indifference from colleagues is actually the least of anyone's concerns. It is rather more disconcerting to have colleagues who gets too intimate or close, crossing the line into personal or private space, and developing relationships that go deeper (and messier) than necessary. When one goes to the office, it is always advisable to repeat this rule like a mantra in the head, time and again, "Trust No One But Yourself", for it is the surest way to curb yourself from troubling consequences.

It is not wise to trust even the nicest, friendliest, most helpful person in the office, even when there is certainly no ill will coming from the other party; because the circumstances have made it as such that this nice person, like everyone else who signed up for a job, has the utmost priority that tends towards selfish purpose: to stay in the job, and bring in the dough. Therefore, no matter how much goodwill the person has for you, it can never supersede this priority; and the circumstances can sometimes jokingly put you and that person to contention. Or you never know if the person has a loose lip that can innocuously let slip of private information that you shared.

Some 'safe trust' is definitely a healthy thing. Dynamic team who works well with interdependent contributions tend to have a good amount of 'safe trust' amongst the team members in getting the work done and achieving their goals. But that doesn't mean that one should cross the line and trust anyone absolutely with sharing of information, especially if the details are too private, personal, controversial, or have the likelihood to get one into trouble. For you may never know the moment when this information will be used against you when contentious occasions arise, even from that nice 'buddy' whom you make the blood pact with at the workplace; because most waged individuals have selfish priorities that supersede everything else.

Other aspects of trust issue we can discuss about, are the blind faith and trust for the organization and/or sweet promises from the superiors. I have mentioned before that everyone in the organization can be equally dispensable when they run out of value, so it is certainly foolish when one pledges absolute loyalty and trust on a machine that only cares about profiteering. Bosses and people in the management frequently employs 'Carrot and Stick' approach on subordinates to sell them a promise of an illusive dream, be it promotions, increments, recommendations and/or acknowledgements. More often so it is a tactic to serve as an impetus for the employee to work harder, and often do not necessarily translate into any tangible benefits, as goal posts can be easily shifted or that superior can simply play amnesiac.

Therefore, trust no one but yourself. But when you cannot even trust yourself, you can outsource to a religion and put your trust in God.

Get Used to
Prejudice and Bias

People at the end of the day have their own sets of preferences and dislikes, and it is unlikely that anyone is truly objective. Therefore, an employee should accept the fact that prejudices and biases exist in the workplace, and it can very much be due to a lot of things: be it one's personality, outlook, gender, race, religion, political inclinations; and a person can even get disliked just based on how he or she walks, talks and breathes.

The modern corporate system has been trying very hard to clamp down and persecutes individuals who actively practice discrimination against more significant areas like races, gender and religion; not for the sake of inclusivity for world peace, but rather to prevent hijacks on their globalist reach and social images.

Yet it is unlikely that such measures will change a thing on the rampant acts of discriminations already happening at the work environment, especially if it is not obviously sexist, racist or bigoted. Humans are complex creatures, and while there are 101 reasons to like a person, there are bound to be detractors and antagonists out there who will dislike somebody for whatever reasons. As a rule of thumb, the employee should not take such actions personally because it is simply human nature.

Prejudice and bias can be felt readily early when a person joins a company. There will be sets of prying eyes and continual assessments to see how a new person can fit into an existing group with its own set of distinct culture, behavior and work ethics; and if the new person falls out of favor, he or she can be actively discriminated against.

Sometimes people can either like or dislike someone's gut almost instantaneously, as if there are already some instinctual code ingrained in the systems that are instantly activated. The colleagues at the group or individual basis form different dynamics with the employee. If one is acceptable, they will have more lunch outings, otherwise expect cold shoulders and social ostracizing.

Likewise, the boss is equally susceptible to such prejudice and bias as well. He or she may show favoritism to a subordinate that is liked better; while sidelining or neglecting another in the process. Sometimes it may be due to work performance, but many times, it can be simply a matter of preference. As such, an employee should never feel discouraged and should just accept the fact that it is just how life works; preferences do change over time, and furthermore, for every hater out there, there is bound to have someone who admire the quality that one possesses, unless the employee is a fundamental gone case.

However, if discrimination goes overboard, especially if it touches on sexism, racism and bigotry, then the situation has turned massively in favor for the victim, because one can play a very epic victim card by getting the attention of HR (Human Resources) to do their corporate obligations to deal with the offender. Most corporations, especially MNCs are very conscious about maintaining a left leaning, diversity embracing social image, and therefore will do whatever they can to stop anyone, even their most valued employees from tarnishing such image.

Things Can Get Nasty

Human nature is inherently evil, and it includes even the nicest people who do things with best intent; because when the condition is right, everyone can revert back to the basic bitch mode. The office is a contentious environment: the power dynamics, the competitions, the work delegations, and conflict of personalities are fertile grounds ripe for conflict situations. On the more overt front, there will be outright aggression; on the more covert end, there are secret sabotage.

Let's talk about the most obvious form of nastiness in the office: Bullying. Hierarchies exist, therefore power dynamics also exist. Some humans are simply mean to other humans whom they perceive as weaker, especially if they themselves are in certain positions of power and authority, with certain ideas of superiority (due to their insecurities). They will gladly bully the weaker counterparts when opportunities arise to press them down further by abuse, threats, intimidations, harassments, and other aggressive actions, as well as forming in-group/out-groups and other power plays.

Bullies tend to have a more choleric and go-getter disposition, yet while most of them are oppressive to subordinates, they smartly play sycophants to superiors. Because of this, they can climb up pretty quick in rank unless they are successfully hijacked by detractors for reporting the bullying.

Then comes another form of nastiness in the office: Character Assassination. The reason why it can thrive very well in the office, is because there are always constant demand for gossips and rumors by the bored office denizens, especially about another person they know; and the nastier those rumors are, the more exciting it is to add color to their boring lives.

There may be some colleagues who did not seem willing to partake (out of moral pretention) but I bet most of them are secretly listening and relishing in the tales. Every Homo sapiens are made of curiosity and bitchiness.

The mouths will gladly carry tales which may or may not have basis on reality, intentionally or not. Many times, especially when done intentionally, the words have the capacity to kill, especially if they concern negative things about a person's character or reputation; words can carry more damage than outright physical harm, because a victim can have reputation tainted indefinitely.

The aforementioned character assassination by gossips and rumors are part of the schemes of covert nastiness. Covert nastiness is something which cannot be obviously seen or witnessed, while damages are already secretly inflicted. Backstabbings and sabotages are other covert acts which can take place quite rampantly in the work environment, especially when there are some levels of competition involved.

While things can get nasty in the workplace, it is important to understand what rights one has as an employee and if the nasty has crossed the line. No matter how bad the nasties are, it is imperative to never lose one's cool in the face of adversaries, because any initiator of anger and physical reactions are instantly penalized and condemned as the wrong party by the blindly unfair "employee protections" of the company.

Understandably, the average employee may be stuck in a situation whereby it is impossible to act on unacceptable behaviors that happen to them, but it doesn't hurt to collect evidence, which can be useful against the offender at some point in time. One may even want to exploit the "employee protections" machinery to play back at their own game. Make complains, and escalate when possible.

On a sidenote, an employee should always actively protect his or her reputation at all cost, as this is one thing that can truly disadvantage a person in the longer run, much more so than the mere altercations in the office.

You Do Not Owe Anyone a Living

Following universal laws of entropy, what can fail will fail and fall apart. Shit is always certain to happen in the office and people cramped together will get on one another's nerves eventually; work performance and results do also go into the trough in every business cycle. So in a way, problems are imminent, but how you handle them will have very drastically different consequences.

As a word of advice, there must be a limit to how seriously you take the job; if it starts to affect your well being, then it is simply not worth it. Because no one will be accountable to you but yourself, and you would have missed out entirely on the bigger picture on why you are here in the first place. The negative emotions that are picked up during negative events can affect both mental and physical health, and will exactly detract you from your purpose (improve life).

Remember, you do not owe anyone a living, and therefore there is no need to beat yourself up if you do not live up to performance the few times for the company (they use you to make money, and if they lose the opportunity to make some money, it is not your fault; those corporations are still filthy rich anyway), or suffer injustice from anyone who want to forfeit your rights; if it happens, the HR is only a corridor away. You are obliged to have a job, but not obliged to its evil; having a certain amount of detachment and cynical optimism will certainly help you along the way. Below are some perspectives which will give you some clarity about what you are into.

1. The reason why you do the job is to better your personal or family life. Getting damaged by a job detract you from your original purpose.

2. Worries add dividends to problems which tend not to be that serious when it happens. Anxiety and embittered grudges are life-quality killers.

3. Except for felonies (which is a grave offence) and misdemeanor, there is no trouble too great which may happen at work: be it missed deadlines, failure to achieve targets, getting into the bad books of some people, etc, because this too soon shall pass. (*although you should protect your reputation at all costs, because notoriety lives forever).

4. When such bad things happen, except for the ephemeral unpleasantry, no one really bothers about you or those incidences several years down the road because people are just getting busy with their own affairs.

5. There is no need to take insults or failures in a company too personally, because no one really cares.

6. That being said, there are of course dangers at the work place, which you can cleverly avoid by using the right tactics and having the right mindset but most of these dangers usually do not amount to real physical dangers, just mere annoyances and inconveniences. The very worst thing that can happen is simply to lose the job. When you lose a job, it can even be a blessing in disguise, because it may open up to new opportunities. If unemployment persists, there are certain strategies that might help you get out of these situations as well.

Many times, in our darkest hours, the pain seem all too real and painful, but they too soon shall pass. I know of many people who often recount unpleasant events from the past with certain relief, sometimes even making a joke out of them.

A Personal Valuation

We have discussed the four 'Real Values' that companies like to look out for; now we should turn inward and examine what values do the employees give themselves. Provided that one has already been hired for a job; this necessarily already prove one thing- that this person deserves the job (I know there are cases of wrong job fits, or just a lucky break for the guy, but that's beside the point). But you need more than that.

Since the day one at work, the employee will be continually assessed by the multitude of eyes in the office, on how the person will fare for the rest of the stay in the company. He or she is constantly watched and monitored, not just by the watchful eyes of the boss, but more so by contenders and detractors on whether the initial valuation is proven correct, and if there is room for growth and development (which they hope not to see). There will also be chances to attract the eyes of patrons and benefactors who can recognize your values.

It will serve you well to first look at your skill sets to see how your own values can value-add to your organization; and how to showcase them, with clearly defined goals on steps towards getting recognitions, good appraisals, promotions, increments, and even creating milestones in your career.

Some people have skills that others don't have; there is no point in comparison, but rather evaluation; to play up existing skills and to downplay potential flaws. Different jobs require different skills (specifically sales job requires good verbal and business negotiation skills, quality assurance job requires good attention to details), but make sure that the job you sign up for matches what you can offer. If you do not have the necessary skill set, either change your job or improve on the skill. Additional skills may or may not further augment career progression; it is good to have a set of specific skills for the specific career that you are intending to carve out, or how it may help you fare in your current role.

Knowing what values you can bring to the company, especially when they sorely lack these features, is your bargaining chip for benefits, entitlements and sustainability. For example, if your company is lacking in people who can talk well, your gift of gab can serve to make you bring much sought after value to the company.

As part of continuous evaluation, one should also have short and long term plans within the job, beyond the company, and in the whole career. One should very well know at some point what value they can offer, whether one is shortchanged or overpaid accordingly to market expectations, on whether one should continue to remain in the organizations with values that can be appreciated by better paymasters. The understanding of your value and worth goes a long way; beyond the mediocre jobs that you may be doing right now, because they have an effect on your life choices and development.

The Key to Survival

Charles Darwin, famed naturalist who contributed to the theories of evolution, once famously said, "It is not the strongest of the species that survives, nor the most intelligent; it is the one most adaptable to change." We can see that happening in natural history, and we can also apply it often in the human context.

Brawn and brains certainly have their own advantages, but if we put all the jocks and nerds from your school days together, how many of them are highly successful in their career today? Probably a handful, and probably not over-represented by either categories, because the reason for their successes are usually nothing to do with their brawn or brains.

I guess most people are inclined to believe that the brainier ones are more advantageous, but I have seen my fair share of smart people getting done in by their overconfidence. That likely reason for the success we brought up earlier largely has to do with **adaptability**.

Adaptability is not just a mutable approach, but a strength and intelligence in itself. It is the ability to adjust to new conditions which are brought about by change. Change is constant, regardless of whether it takes place in the workplace or in other aspects of life, and while it is definitely certain, progress is not. To be able to adjust to changes, the strength lies in the forbearance to withstand being shifted out of the comfort zone and to deal with the unpleasant part of changes, the tenacity to not give up on new challenge, the resolve to plan and strategize; and the intelligence lies in the sagacity to accept that adaptation when faced with change is the key to success, the foresight to read and plan situations before it happens, the perspicacity to read and act according to situations when it happens.

Adaptability as the key to survival at the very least will enable a person to face and mitigate many troubles and problems at work, prepare for 'black swan events' (i.e. sudden surprises at work), and sustain employment posterity.

Adaptability when used at a more dynamic and ambitious level can open the doors to new opportunities, allowing the person to scale new heights, and get into favorable positions in the career. The lack of adaptability often spells the downfall of many wasted talents; it could be due to their stubbornness, overconfidence, unwillingness to compromise, or simply lack of flexibility to handle situations. The wasted talent is one of life's greatest tragedy, more so than the most mediocre person.

As a key to survival, if the person doesn't already have it, it is not the easiest skill to attempt. The combination of the aforementioned strength and intelligence require a certain degree of open-mindedness and the willingness to learn, the ability to put down one's ego for long term goals. Perhaps it is time to sit down and contemplate what are the things you want to achieve in life, and examine how you had been handling things so far, and then see how things could have turned out differently if you changed approach and applied adaptability.

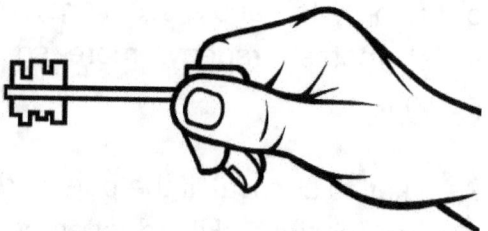

The many suggestions I shared in this book can only be effectively carried out by the adaptable person. It is not too late to start now.

2. Knowledge and Propriety

Humans are instinctively social creatures, and many will find themselves conforming to a social standard as part of group survival strategy. When humans get together, there are usually rules set in place. Rules (and laws) are created because each and every individual, while gathered together in a group for common purposes, have ultimately different personality, objectives and behavior, which may actually do the group a disservice if they fall out of line.

In order not to get into trouble in a company, it is critical to understand and observe its rules, both written and unspoken; and knowing the people, dynamics, situations and acting accordingly. "Knowledge" is power, and it can enable one to avoid making grave transgressions against these set expectations and/or to mitigate the potential pitfalls and entrapments for a safer passage in the career.

Observe and understand the hierarchy, the team dynamics, the legalities, the culture, and look beyond the veneer of what is obvious and catch the subtlety amid the smiles and handshakes for any hidden motivations, signs of discontent and other deep politics in the organization. With this knowledge, the shrewd employee can use it to his/her advantage by pretending to conform to the company's code of conduct (although there are really impressionable ones who can actually get indoctrinated and entrenched by this code of conduct), and also to handle the colleagues well.

Regardless of whether the employee agrees with the rules (laws) of the company or not, he/she is wise to act and behave in a way that the company and its people find acceptable. This is the strategy termed as "Propriety", and it is not just a pragmatic way (pretending or not) to behave accordingly, say and do the right things and stay in line, but also the stoic practice of cultivating caution, control of emotions, and strategic mind-set. Falling short of Propriety can greatly disadvantage an employee. Because it could be used to wrongfully imply the lack of loyalty or efficiency of the person; and this can even often bring highly competent employees down, due to such mis-step. Also, in the other chapters, we discuss "The Art of Concealment", and "Projecting the Right Image". These are extensions of the Propriety, but first we need to get to the bottom of knowing it right before doing it right.

Otto von Bismarck once mentioned a famous line, "Only a fool learns from his own mistakes. The wise man learns from the mistakes of others." Take your time to observe and learn. You will surely see some fumble, stumble and tumble along the way. Do not be that person; the sacrificial lamb or scapegoat to the slaughter by being ignorant or oblivious to the complex code of conduct in the organization. Be wise as serpent; keep calm and observe.

You Will Always Be Watched

The fact is somewhat uncomfortable, but most employees are constantly watched and assessed. Most of the time, it may not even be obvious to the employee, because those who are watching will not explicitly stare at anyone. The monitoring can come from all places in all manners, like a brief glimpse at you, the color of your Skype status, your Powerpoint presentations, your results.

I have mentioned elsewhere before that the moment a person joins the company, he or she will be assessed continually by a multitude of eyes, from the boss to the co-workers, from allies and detractors alike: for profiling, mistakes, threats, etc. On a pettier note, one can also be constantly watched for punctuality, job attendance, work attitude, tea breaks, and the internet sites surfed (yes IT department has ability to do that).

Therefore, one of the very important reminder that readers should heed in "Knowledge and Propriety" is to be conscious of the fact that you are watched, therefore do behave appropriately. Big Brother (boss, management) is definitely watching because they frequently have discussions about staff assessments with the HR. Watch your behavior, your manners, and your activities constantly and make sure that they do not fall out of line with propriety, as someone will definitely be taking notes, be it Big Brother or the snitches.

Understand the
Reasons of Your Hire

There is usually a 'strong' reason why an employee gets hired, because hiring is a tedious and resource consuming process for the company. Is your immediate boss looking to expand his or her operations to make the work easier, or the company more profitable? Is your position a newly created role, or a replacement? Do you get a sense that you are hired against the will of your boss, due to pressure from upper management? Do you feel that your position could be a threat to your immediate boss? These are very important factors that can determine how your boss will potentially view and treat you in your job.

If you are a hire for a newly created position to help your boss expand work capability, you are usually in pretty favorable position with the boss, because your presence might probably improve the standing of your boss in terms of 'getting additional support' by making the work closer to success, or 'adding to the headcount' of the platoon, so he and her can flaunt the strength of the team to boost the ego and the associated false sense of pride and security. Also, as mentioned before, a newly created position is likened to an 'experiment', therefore there is more room for failure, but this can turn pretty bad if you are hired to be a 'miracle worker' to solve long-standing problems, although the chances are low.

If you are hired as a replacement, there is a chance that the immediate boss 'can be' problematic, assuming that the problem did not lie with your predecessor. Normally when someone leaves the job, it tends to be due to 'problems'. There is no such thing as leaving the job feeling 'happy and satisfied' with the ex-employer, because if that was really the case, the person wouldn't need to leave the job and venture out. It could be due to many reasons, like dissatisfaction, lack of appreciation, work pressure, office politics and toxicity from colleagues, etc.

If the last employee left on their own accord (resigned), chances are, the problems might be somehow linked to the boss. In a more direct way, the boss could be hard to work with, display toxic behavior, behave oppressively or set unrealistic expectations, constantly sideline the individual, miserly on promotions and increments, etc. Or the boss may indirectly contribute to the departure, by sheer incompetence, on the losing side in the office politics arena, or inability to garner power to help the employee.

And assuming that the last employee was fired, the 'red flag' is now hoisted much higher, because that makes the boss even more dangerous, and it could imply that he or she may be pretty demanding and trigger happy, which then spells imminent pressure and stress. Hence, in any circumstances, being a replacement always has its associated risks; with a very high likelihood that the 'miracle worker' expectation is usually in place for this type of employee.

If the employee is hired against the will of the boss, then the odds are usually stacked ever higher against the employee. Assuming that a position needs to be filled because the management demanded so, the boss will relent to do the 'needful' for this hire, but otherwise act neglectful, disdainful or condescending towards this individual, unless the person turns out to be a useful and helpful subordinate.

However, if the employee is 'recommended' by someone higher up than the boss, then the dynamics is shifted further. The boss will usually feel paranoid about this employee and will act extra diplomatic/courteous and attentive, but at the same time hold extreme contempt, suspicion, and would constantly pray that this employee will perish and cease to exist because one can't shake off the feeling that this employee might be a spy from the upper management, or a potential replacement for oneself.

The worst scenario is when the boss perceives that the employee is created as a potential threat to his/her position. One way an employee can get a sense of that is when the hire is not initiated by the immediate boss (foisted by management), and/or job responsibilities or the level of the title of the position is somewhat 'close' to the boss (for example, the employee with the title regional sales manager and the boss with the title senior sales manager).

When that happens, it is almost certain that the immediate boss will give hell, in overt or covert manner to the employee, provided that if he or she did not get upset enough to quit the job in the first instance.

Be Familiar with the Legalities and Policies of The Company

Before we even go on, first read your employment contract and understand every terms and conditions. Look out for fine prints, especially in parts that are potentially dangerous, like negligence, non-competition clause, moonlighting policies, non disparagement and compensations. Almost every parts are written to protect the interest of the company in case an employee goes rogue, or when they need an excuse to boot the person.

And when you are finally in the job, you still need to be careful about employee conduct and ethics, compliance, confidentiality and non-disclosure, security and equal opportunity. Most of these policies are largely the same across most companies, but there may be some deviations. The last thing that any employee wants to happen is to be legally implicated during employment or thereafter.

If your job involves making or signing contracts for customers or businesses, then be extra careful, because these are more varied and prone to errors than just abiding to fixed policies of the companies; be very certain about the terms, signatories, especially if you are in charge of making them, or signing them.

Understand and Act out
The Ethics of the Profession

The policies are one thing, but there are also corporate standards of behavior not written on paper. When we last discussed about company 'Core Values' in "What Companies Really Care About", many of these short taglines are ciphers for ethics, which consist of these virtues: honesty, integrity, transparency, accountability, confidentiality, objectivity, respect, obedience to the law, and loyalty. Anyone *really* having all these qualities are not of this mortal world, therefore do not beat yourself up if you cannot uphold all of them, especially loyalty (and do not kid yourself in believing you have all of them, otherwise you will not be reading this book).

Ethics is however more than virtue in itself. It is also a weapon of choice in the workplace. While it is true that no one is perfect, the employee is expected to act his or her part. If the person shows an obvious display of behavior or action antithetical to the aforementioned ethics, and these somehow gets documented as evidence, then this person will likely get black marked, censured or even booted, depending on the severity of the incidents. Therefore, always be mindful of ethics, and act the careful part.

Observing the Company
And the Office Culture

When a person joins a new organization, he or she is always likely to get "Culture Shock", whether in a big or small way, even if the company is from a similar industry like the last, or having familiar faces and previously known acquaintances. Because it is always certain that cliques had been formed, habits had been set, and culture had evolved in the department, and the addition of this new employee is often seen as a disruption to the status quo, unless the environment is a newly created one. The new employee without a clue, now immersed in uncharted territories, has to find a way to survive seeing the new faces, and interacting with them, for quite a while.

Before signing up for the work offer, it is always prudent to do the homework on what kind of company one is applying for (try Glassdoor website); investigate, snoop around, dig for rumors and gossips on the organization. This information will be extremely invaluable, as they can often inform the culture of the company for a job hunter to make his or her assessment of the company and to prepare and set expectations on this new endeavor. The truth is company cultures can differ from one place to the other. A very obvious example of different company cultures can be observed between American, European and Asian companies. American: dynamic and aggressive, European: laidback and steadfast, Asian: bureaucratic and regimental. However, most of the companies in the world are now pushing towards a more American corporate culture.

After getting familiar with the company culture, the next thing to be even more familiar with is the office culture. For any newcomer to a workplace, it always pays to behave in a modest, low profile manner; listening more than speaking unnecessarily. Over a week or two, the newcomer will have an overview on the general culture of the environment; like their attitude and habits (although colleagues may be putting up a brief show before they lapse back into original ways), how long the lunchtime breaks are, general vibe in the air (gloomy or cheerful), etc.

Slightly over 2 weeks into the job, the newcomer may learn more about the interpersonal dynamics between colleagues, boundaries, potential friends and enemies. Within 2 months into the job, alliances would have been forged (unless you're a loner), and one may get a pretty good sense about the politics in the office.

Knowing the Hierarchy

Similar to the animal kingdom, human beings are also packed in social hierarchy wherever they are, and the workplace is no exception. In a corporation, the CEO is usually the king of the hill. And then there will be branches extended downwards into senior management, middle management, so on and so forth. The top dogs in the company are usually primed from the business, finances and/or operations lines, and the rest tend to be branched sideways from the peripheries. Different lines serve different business functions, and somewhere along the line, the employee will be placed therein with a boss above, and with subordinates below if any.

The hierarchy is strictly observed in all companies, even in the flattest, leanest organization, because somebody has to obviously take charge and call the shots. Starting at the level above the employee, the immediate boss (or supervisor) is someone that the employee needs to be accountable to. This immediate boss also has his or her own boss to report to.

Every company observes the 'chain of command'. In an organizational structure, it refers to a company's hierarchy of reporting relationships – from the bottom to the top of an organization, who must answer to whom. The chain of command not only establishes accountability, it lays out a company's lines of authority and decision-making power. One of the very important rules in this chain is that the employee should not skip the immediate boss to a higher authority during reporting.

This is a major transgression that not only upsets the structure set in place, but also upsets the immediate boss. Every supervisors by default are paranoid and usually do not entertain the idea of his or her subordinate talking to his or her boss. The more forthcoming supervisor will surely censure the employee; the more insidious types present much greater danger. It is therefore important to strictly observe this rule unless one is planning a revolt.

At the same time, one should know very well the person who can be very crucial to your successes- the boss of the boss. No immediate boss in the world is keen to actively promote a staff who will one day undermine his or her authority. When promotions are allowed to happen, the immediate boss is usually promoted as well.

But there are a great amount of immediate bosses who do not even want to risk promoting the subordinates at all, and therefore will continually pass up all chances of promoting the person. When that happens, the savior can turn out to be the boss of the boss, whom the employee should cautiously try to get close to, and strategically influence to gain favor from, for that chance to go up in ranks. This of course is a rather risky endeavor but it is part of the strategy that I will offer at a later part in the book.

The Old Boys Club

This term is used loosely to describe either the senior management, or an office community of powerful employees. There are also increasingly more 'Old Girls Club' as we speak, and they are all the same. They are the group that set unwritten rules in the company, that have the power and authority to set political precedence, and they tend to be gated, opening up to worthy compadre, or shutting off from further admittance.

When you get into a company, aside from your Boss, you will notice that they are the people that you'd need to watch out for, because they wield considerable power that can either help or destroy you.

The most prominent of the 'Old Boys Club', the senior management, is a tier in the upper echelon of office politics, whereby the incumbents care more about upkeeping their status, image and power, than to really care about what is happening below them. They may still care enough about driving the 'company vision', but it is usually for selfish motivations like glories and rewards.

They can be incompetent at work but they surely have the smarts and perspectives which normal hardworking folks do not have. Here is a breakdown on what are the things that may get one admittance to the Old Boys (or Girls) Club:

1. **Preference is a subjective human behavior, which occurs in all human beings.** The top guys in the company, like everyone else, have certain likes and dislikes. In order for the more senior guy to accept an employee into management, that senior guy must firstly, like the employee. 'Like' in this case is not solely about personal liking although it can include that. It is mostly: a) same political affiliation- meaning to say, on his side in office politics, b) subordination- the person has to observe the top guy as the higher guy, respecting the authority, c) value- the person can help the top guy consolidate and expand power, spread influence, improve work function, and add to his credentials.

2. **People in the management tend to be generalist than specialist.** They may even be mediocre and/or incompetent in actual work. However, they have several skill sets that are highly valuable for their corporate ladder climb:

   a) Verbal skills- the ability to express well. It doesn't just means the gift of the gab, but rather it is the ability to influence, convince and excite.

   b) Understanding of human nature- the ability to watch cues and behave accordingly. There is a part of the knowledge economy that is more invaluable than information, and that is observations of human dynamics and behavior.

c) Networking- having verbal skills and human understanding are not enough if the candidate do not actively seek out to interact with the top dogs. This part takes certain extroversion and thick skin, but the results can be startlingly impressive. Even if the top dogs sense insincerity from such attempts, they relent and even appreciate and like it because the top dogs like affirmation of their power, to have underdogs licking their boots and other attempts at brown nosing.

d) Opinions- in the knowledge economy, and with the surfeit of information, many information may not even be accurate or true (e.g. fake news). However, attempts to seem clever, insightful or creative, even when they are not, often successfully hoodwink and impress the top dogs, because these guys don't know any better. As long as ideas (that align to the values of the management or organization) are enthusiastically brought up, they tend to be treated as a fresh breath when in reality they are bullshits.

e) Leverage- the average person who can do management are maybe not so good in specialized work area, but they sure as hell can leverage. It can be getting someone else (usually the specialists) to do the work for you, and then getting all the credits thereafter. This is the reason why sometimes the people in management are much hated, but they surely don't mind that, and even credit it as one of the smarts of textbook leadership skills.

Knowing the Boss

Much of the boon or bane to an employee's prospect in the company lies with the boss, the immediate supervisor, the direct reporting line. Therefore, it is important to know the boss, so one can plan, act and behave accordingly.

The psyche of the boss is usually the same, regardless of the vast differences in personality, race or creed, across the different industries and different parts of the world.

And that is: while they expect you to do these: serve, solve problems, boost image, add to strength so they can have influence and power over their competitions, they also hope that you will not do better than themselves (and especially if you manage to catch the attention of his or her boss), will not do too badly to jeopardize their portfolio, will not conspire against them (most bosses are paranoid about this), will not pull a fast one and give them nasty surprises like quitting all of a sudden, or go missing in action.

Of course, there are nice bosses of agreeable nature, but even they frequently have those insecurities. The wise, empathetic and caring bosses we sometimes hear about are usually people who already have reasonable amount of successes in life (mind you not just career, but overall in life), and probably did the job out of boredom, or hold enviable positions in the company. The average bosses, even if they have 'nice' qualities, can easily turn green-eyed or see red when they deem their subordinates capable of stealing their thunder, or upsetting their status quo. On the other spectrum, we have the bosses from hell, like the slave drivers, histrionic wrecks or worse still, the psychopathic manipulators.

The key to surviving the company is to be on the favorable side of the immediate boss. If the immediate boss gives you hell, it can be detrimental to your well being, regardless of whether you have the resilience to bear his/her ill treatment, because bad things can be set up behind your back without your knowledge. Generally, if you abide by these rules of engagement with the boss, chances to survive or thrive are higher:

1. Do not bring trouble or problem to the boss.
2. Do not bring too much bad news to the boss.
3. Complete assigned tasks on time.
4. Do work that will make the boss looks good.
5. Do not complain or seek too much help from the boss.
6. Do not steal the boss's thunder.
7. Toe the line. Seem transigent, respect the boss's authority as a superior.
8. Stay away from the boss's superior or enemies.
9. To be on the side of the boss in the political game.

And while you are still on the favorable side of the boss, it is prudent to set up contingency plans, like networking with other colleagues, secretly establishing links between yourselves and the immediate bosses' superior (you've got to be very careful with this one) or key personnel in the company, because things can easily go south very fast; you may be an apple turned rotten in the eye of the boss for any misgivings, real or imagined, from his or her perspectives due to unforeseen circumstances beyond your control.

You probably already get a sense of what sort of person the immediate boss is going to be like when you turn up for interviews, or hear his/her voice over the phone if you did not have a physical meet-up. Nevertheless, first impressions can still be inaccurate and sometimes deceiving, because people tend to act polite, diplomatic or even charming on first encounter.

Do make use of the tips in the book on profiling, reading people and cues, to try to form a picture of the person you are dealing with. Then read the different tactics and strategies to learn how to deal with the boss accordingly.

Knowing the Colleagues

Beside knowing the boss, it is important for the employee to also know the colleagues. These are the people the employee will frequently need to interact with, either from the same team, or within the same office. The colleagues may or may not have the same job function as the employee, but their effects on the well being of the employee are profound. Their influences are much more direct, frequent and long term than the reporting line, or with other departments because they are a constant company frequently revolving around the working life of the employee.

Within the office community, you will find that you are dealing with people from all walks of life; with interests, personality, motivations and values that can be very dissimilar to yours, and who may or may not like you. Yet you may also find out that there is an underlying collective cultural behavior, attitude and practices that define this community; with unspoken rules which are set in precedence that is unique to this group.

Therefore, one of the very important measure for an employee to take is to find out and learn to adapt to the culture of this group, an advice which has been touched on earlier in the chapter. The very next step is to handle each and every colleagues on a more personal basis because these people can turn out to be friends, foe, or just neutral employees who just happen to hang around in the close proximity (touched on later in the chapter). The employee should always take care not to fall out of favor with powerful colleagues, or the collective, because they can surely make working life difficult; which can range from just getting ignore and ostracized, to getting sabotaged.

In this book, I had discussed at great lengths about the different ways to profile people, tactics to use on a day to day basis, as well as long term strategies to ensure a successful stay in the job. The key really lies in understanding people, picking up the right cues and behaving appropriately. In order to survive the corporation and the intricate political games played, it is important to learn well to deal with them accordingly, forming a thorough understanding of collaegues as a collective and as individuals, their personality traits, likes and dislikes, goals and motivations, how they view you, their power and influence within the company, and then subsequently identify the presence and dynamics of political factions which they may partake in.

Knowing the
Other Departments

When an employee is placed within a department, his or her primary role is to help address or fulfil the function of that department. This function is not likely to be autonomous, and may require certain checks and balances, as well as getting apportioned as a cog to a part of a process mechanism that involve other departments.

The department is networked to other departments to make its function more efficient and assured. The employee may or may not be immediately accountable to the other departments per se, but the department, as well as its heads are likely liable to be accountable to them. Generally, a department is interacting with five other departments, generally classified as a) counterparts, b) regulator, c) giver, d) recipient and e) connector.

1. **Counterparts**- This department corresponds to or has the same function as your department in a different place or situation. If you are in the IT department that does internal service support for the company, a counterpart will be either an IT department that does external customer facing service support, or is based in other locations that do exactly the same function. Counterpart departments are usually viewed as equivalents, but can get contentious (usually between

departmental heads) if there are other comparisons been made or when job functions are overlapped.

2. **Regulators**- This department corresponds to one that is in charge of setting guidelines, auditing, or regulating your department. If you are in the business development department which actively positions tech regulated product at different markets, the regulators will be your tech regulatory department as well as trade compliance department who would assess and control the entry of these products to the market, in accordance to the region's policies and regulations. Regulator departments are usually viewed as meddlesome, a function is significantly slowed down due to these activities.

3. **Givers**- This department provides support and assistance to your business unit. If you are in the corporate communications department, the legal department will be your giver, who will help the department to vet through press releases prior to release to the public. Giver department is usually viewed as beneficial, as it renders services that are much needed by the recipient.

4. **Recipients**- This department gets support and assistance from your business unit. If you are in the marketing department, you will continuously provide support through collaterals, marketing and lead generation for the sales department, which is a recipient department. Recipient department is usually

not viewed favorably, as they are always seemingly at cross purposes, and viewed as demanding to the supporters.

5. **Connectors**- This department may sit at the periphery but somehow is linked to every other department. Examples are the human resources department, and even the cleaners who might have frequent interactions with most of the office denizens at every cubicles and corners of the office. The Connector departments are usually viewed with less importance by other departments, although they are probably the best source for getting first-hand information and rumor in the company.

The five departments can sometimes have overlaps. Nevertheless, it is important to know the five departments interacting with your department, for they are not just crucial for the understanding of the inter-departmental dynamics, but also a possible source of valuable information that is not normally dispensed to your business unit, or even a breeding ground for political assemblage should matter not goes so well within your department (especially if that departmental leader you have trouble with is an unpopular figure in the eyes of the other departments).

It doesn't hurt to pop by and chit chat with colleagues from other departments and establish relationships; you'd be surprised to find out how much you can benefit from this exercise.

Assessing Professional Profiles on LinkedIn

One way to assess the boss (or fellow colleagues) is to look at the information which are readily accessible to you; via the internet. Most professionals these days have a (or several) LinkedIn accounts. It doesn't hurt to do a name search on LinkedIn and see the profile of your immediate boss (or any colleagues that you care to spy on). Most LinkedIn profiles are set to public anyway, and usually full of information on the career history as they are intended to attract potential recruiters as well as to show off the capability of the person.

1. **Duration of stay in past jobs**- The duration of stay in a company can sometimes show whether a person is in it for the long haul or short hops. The general thing about the long hauler is that they tend to be more stable, steadfast personality. If the long hauler stays on in the company with very few changes to his or her job responsibility, then this person is likely not as ambitious nor appreciated, yet just stick around for a long time.

If the long haulers frequently get promotions year after year in the same company, this person is probably a star employee. The long haulers usually like order and structure, or 'stability' and tend to be more competent. This kind of boss is usually good to have around, and if the boss moves on up the ranks, chances are you will be pulled upwards along; but if he or she is stagnating in the company, this also applies accordingly.

In the case of the job-hopping type, they tend to mean both good and bad news. Starting with the bad first: they may be extremely opportunistic, incompetent or political.

The worst is the latter, whereby every company has the potential to be wrecked by this person, who likely burn bridges and other acts of proverbial felonies. This type of boss however don't tend to stay long, and therefore if you work under the boss, you will tend to have more opportunities for growth, especially if you do your work better than him/her.

2. **Recommendations**- This is the part on LinkedIn where the users get testimonials from superiors, subordinates, colleagues, business associates, or friends. Quite often, these may be just mutual social endorsements arranged between the user and agreeing party in the connections, but even that is quite a feat in itself (shows that the person is quite smart in networking and building rapport).

Take note of how many recommendations are received and given. If the person has received more than given, he or she may indeed be competent. However, if the given recommendations are lacking, this may also go to show that the user is quite self serving. On the other hand, if the given ones are much more than received recommendations, then this person may be failing in the little social rapport game, lacking in reciprocity from most of the other recipient and may show the lack of popularity of this professional.

3. **Education**- Users on LinkedIn are required to put in their highest education qualification level and where they received their education, Ivy League or not. Most users who had at least went through college usually don't see the need to include details about their middle schools, unless there are reasons to brag (elite, privileged schools).

If the person has a doctorate education, and includes PhD after the name or has Dr/Prof prefix before the name on LinkedIn profile, it is also another way of bragging. The people who do the aforementioned tend to be insecure, status conscious and harp on past glories (probably their one shot at fame). Same thing with the types who include Mensa membership, they are also likely to be intellectual snobs to some degree.

Another thing to look for at the education profile: the college (and beyond) names and qualifications. Select, copy, paste on a Google search engine and search, and see where it leads you to. In my experience, a LinkedIn user with more than 200 contacts will be able to find one contact with dubious college qualification= likelihood of a degree mill.

4. **Activities**- The fantastic thing about LinkedIn these days is that it is pretty much like Facebook, albeit for professionals. That means people can write posts, comments and give 'likes'. In this current age of social media, the users frequently run the risk of unknowingly exposing flaws and weaknesses which normally wouldn't surface in the past, potentially contributed from the complacency or tomfoolery of treating LinkedIn like Facebook.

If you are a LinkedIn user, you may come across on a day to day basis, some posts or comments from other users that are either mildly inane, to highly controversial, because these 'professionals' are either too keen to express their opinions, or to impress.

Many vocal LinkedIn denizens make motherhood statements on mindless platitude & pointless rhetoric about leadership with follow up comments to the posts usually parroting the same points or saying needless things like 'I agree'. Most of the activities however consist of putting 'likes' on the posts.

There is a section on LinkedIn where you can find all the social activities on that person's profile and here is where you can do your bit of stalking. If you see a user liking many of the posts on career advice (e.g. how a boss should behave better), there is a chance of dissatisfaction with the job.

If this person likes or comments a lot on posts from 'high net worth' professionals beyond their league, he or she is probably trying to stretch networking goals, rather evidently brown nosing, or attempt to elevate status through such associations. You may even find opinions or reactions on controversial topics (feminism, Trump, etc) from the users, and get a sense of their leanings or degree of pretence.

Social and Power Gauges

One needs to have a clear understanding of the social and power status of the Boss and the co-workers in order to thrive better in the office. Aside from official job titles, and duties, you are dealing with real people, and they all have different personality, motivations, and inclinations.

Everyone is a would-be friend, enemy, and partner-in-crime; and these status can change all the time. When things get political or contentious with a person in the company, it is always helpful if you already have a good understanding about the person, on many levels. During peacetime, it is always wise to already start assessing and profiling your co-workers.

1. **Study the Lifestyle**- It is even better if you can get into the person's Facebook or other 'casual' social media profiles, beginning with a name search on Google. Quite often a search result may bring up some information about the person, his or her lifestyle, social exploits, personal interests and relationships, especially if the person has a unique name.

   If you have a John Smith for the person, then extend the keyword search to his affiliations, last companies he worked in, his hometown etc, to filter the results. The results will paint a fair picture of what the person acts like after work; for example, if the person has an artistic side, chances are he or she is less uptight than the plebs into fast cars. See what interests the person, so you can get into the 'soft spots' with the person next time.

Or finding out that the prudish stony faced boss has a secret life as a party animal who get into compromising positions with people- you never know what you may potentially stumble upon in the world of social media.

2. **Feedback from the market**- Anyone involved in a specific industry for longer than 2 years would have garnered some level of reputation, whether commendable, mediocre or notorious. Hear from the people from the industries, from your acquaintances, or even from the people in the new company (this option needs to be cautious) on a general review of the person.

If you are a newcomer to the industry, you can still get some clues from recommendations on LinkedIn profiles, feedbacks from many different recruitment executives (a surprisingly good resource), and very importantly, from the customers in the field.

3. **Assessing the Influence**- Just how powerful is the person? Is he or she a force to be reckoned with or just puppets of higher power? Is the position a testimony of the prowess or merely a titular namesake? You can get a sense of that by the colleagues' treatment of this person. If the boss of the boss even sounded unusually courteous or respectful to this person, then you know that

you have a puissant one. On the other hand, if the subordinates are even brusque or disrespectful to the boss, you know that this person is a boss only in name.

4. **External Dynamics**- These dynamics do not involve yourself, but between the potential person and other people. Take note of how the person interacts with fellow colleagues, superiors or subordinates; is this person brusque to subordinates but sweet and pandering to the superiors? How does this person treat service staff, for example, when you are having meals in a restaurant? Is this person having any say in the presence of other colleagues?

If the person ill treats other people but appears nice to you, then this person may potentially give you problems at some point later. If the person feels uncomfortable in the presence of the other colleagues, then there may be some tensions going on between the individuals or factions within the company. All these are interesting things to observe and make mental notes of.

5. **Behavior**- During the initial meetings, you don't need to be a psychic to figure out what the boss (or other colleagues) are really like, if you can take note of the subtle cues to form a picture of them. For example, if this person occasionally punctuates his or her soft voice abruptly to harsher tone and louder voice to emphasize a point, this person is likely a repressed person with passive aggressive tendencies. If in the initial meetings, the boss is already loud and showing signs of being

histrionic, he or she is likely not a long term performer and may give you plenty of drama.

Look at the gaze, the demeanor and the attitude of the person, is he or she sizing you up or making you feel relaxed? Sometimes you can trust your instincts as inherent warning signs, because nasty people tend to give bad vibes, even if they are smiling like a Cheshire Cat in your encounter.

Watch what the boss says to you during interviews; does he or she sound condescending or sarcastic? Is he or she dropping hints of some potential work problems? Try to catch them and do your assessment.

After the initial meetings, the true color of the boss (or your colleagues) will become apparent as the days go by, and by then it will be too late for the ill prepared. The cordiality and courtesy fades away as soon as they get to business, and in most instances, the behavior usually took a turn for the worse.

Most behavior are pretty harmless, for example, the person may be grouchier, colder, ruder, more impatient as time goes by, but they may also turn out to become horror story villains, wrecking the sanity of the employee.

6. **Assessing the Strengths, Weaknesses and Job Timeline-** At the outset, it is crucial to correctly distinguish the strengths and weaknesses of the person.

Of course this may change over time, but you will get most of ideas right through initial interactions. Sit down and ponder this important question: "how does this person gets the job?"; "how does this person becomes my boss?" And then start to examine what are the qualities which this person possesses.

Depending on the nature of the industry, different skill sets are valued differently. A braggart without credentials or substance can get ahead for making oneself heard. An autist with poor communications can get ahead with special technical expertise.

Distinguish what are the strengths and weaknesses of this person to use to your advantage; then get a sense of how long he or she may get to stay in the organization because of the skills and value contribution.

Opposing Forces
At the Workplace

In every work environment, we can find the interplay of 2 opposing forces, namely the 'Status Quo' and the 'New Order'; at different levels, from the general ethos of the company, down to the individuals driving the forces.

The 'Status Quo', as the name implies, is the protector that is bolstering the upkeep of the old order, to preserve old processes and values.

The 'New Order', as the name implies, is a change agent intent on overthrowing the old order, with the establishment of new standards. The opposing forces can be mutually exclusive or interdependent, depending on how the organization or the individual are normalized.

At the extremes, the two forces are working in opposition, and quite often their interplay become the motion which drives the organization towards a certain characteristic. This characteristic can be entirely dominated by either one force, which will therefore provide the character of the company; whether as a slow moving languid one, or an accelerated chaos-monger, on either pole.

The 2 forces consist of 9 qualities in human dynamics, namely Meta, Ideas, Focus, Communications, Energy, Motivation, Esteem, Compliance, and Interaction.

Meta is a quality concerning the transcendental aspects. It has two types: the Vernacular- which features basal concerns with the material, and the Profound- which features high-mindedness for society, humankind and/or spirituality.

Ideas is a quality concerning the mental aspects. The two types are Conservative- which is averse to change and hold on to traditional values, with a pragmatic subtype, and Progressive- which advocates reforms and innovations, with an idealistic subtype.

Focus is a quality concerning the visual range. The first type is Meticulous- which is a micro view on perspectives, and being careful to details. The second type is Big Pictured- which as the name implies, is having a macro view on perspectives, looking at situations in a holistic manner.

Communications is a quality concerning the verbal aspects. The two types are Reserved- which is slow to reveal emotions or opinions, and Open- which is the opposite; casual in revealing emotions or opinions.

Motivation is a quality concerning the 'professional' social priority. We know that everyone by default is Selfish, but there are cases when group priority can be made in a professional setting (psychology can be complex, some people feel better serving the community to satisfy the ego, which is essentially still selfish). The two types are Individual- which is interest for personal growth, and Group Centric- which is interest for community priority.

Energy is a quality concerning the states of human motions and activities. The two types are Passive- which is at the inert state, and Active- which is at the engaged state.

Esteem is a quality concerning the measure of self worth. There are two types, namely Insecure- affected by self doubt, uncertainty and Confident- having certainty and self assurance.

Compliance is a quality concerning the attitude towards authority. Subservient- yielding, deferential and dutiful. Subversive- rebellious, disruptive and willing to challenge authority.

Interaction is a quality concerning the mode of engagement. Harmonious- cordial, agreeable, amicable, whereas Antagonistic- active opposition and hostility

There are no good or bad with regards to Status Quo vs New Order forces; but rather a marked difference in qualities. The extreme representation of either forces possess clearly defined types of qualities as seen in the table below.

The extreme Status Quo force is Vernacular, Conservative, Meticulous, Reserved, Individual, Passive, Insecure, Subservient and Harmonious.

The extreme New Order force is Profound, Progressive, Big Pictured, Open, Group Centric, Active, Assured, Subversive and Antagonistic.

The 9 Qualities of the Opposing Forces

	Qualities	A. Status Quo	B. New Order
1	Meta	Vernacular	Profound
2	Ideas	Conservative	Progressive
3	Focus	Meticulous	Big Pictured
4	Communications	Reserved	Open
5	Motivation	Individual	Group Centric
6	Energy	Passive	Active
7	Esteem	Insecure	Assured
8	Compliance	Subservient	Subversive
9	Interaction	Harmonious	Antagonistic

The two extreme forces will frequently clash and come into conflict over the values they stand for, and are particularly evident when change agency comes into place.

Imagine an organization with long tradition of stability, growing organically at a slow rate, and populated by workers who are laidback protectors of these values. Then comes a company buyout situation whereby this organization (Status Quo) is acquired and merged into an aggressive, fast growing organization (New Order).

The proponents from the latter company will surely want to implement and enforce their work styles, which may be challenging to the original company, surely causing distress, unhappiness and general upset of the status quo. This type of conflict situation evidently happens a lot of times in many cases of Merger and Acquisitions between companies, Restructuring between departments, and even newcomers into the management.

The forces cited are extremes. In most cases, companies, departments or the co-workers possess a fair mix of different qualities which may see them inclining at varying degrees towards the Status Quo or the New Order characteristics.

Defining the Traits
Of the Co-workers

When it comes to the study of personality types, there are many popular choices like Myers-Briggs Type Indicator (MBTI), DISC Assessment, Enneagram Tests and others. These tests are both appreciated and critiqued, and had substantial support by corporate human resources as tools to profile its staffs. Do check out these tests if you are interested. What we are using here is a different test which makes use of the 9 qualities of the opposing forces to determine common traits.

There are always the Good, the Bad and the Ugly in every organization; most of them are instantly recognizable, from their outlook to their attitude and working style. Most of the Good are recognized for either their agreeable nature or good work. Most of the Bad are obviously obnoxious, difficult and display disagreeable traits. The Ugly are well, a league of their own. However, when the 9 qualities are applied, we are looking at a scenario that is beyond good and evil. It becomes a case of different emphasis of values.

In the world of Rick Lazarus, everyone is selfish by default. Everyone has the potential to become nasty when shit hits the fan. To deal with people, one has to examine what are the values and beliefs one hold, and then see how it can affect the community that one is interacting with. If there are major differences in values, one might have to find ways to either adapt and compromise accordingly, or get out. You can start by testing your 9 qualities assessment and see where you stand. If your qualities align with the company you are working for, it is a good start. Then work on your Boss/colleagues.

To begin, first look at the table on the 9 Qualities of the Opposing Forces. The nine qualities have two outcomes: either A. Status Quo, or B. New Order. Write an honest assessment about the qualities that were observed.

Example: Graham the Accountant that you've been secretly observing –

Vernacular under Meta because he generally only cares about the practical aspects of life.

Conservative under Ideas as he prefers to play safe.

Meticulous under Focus because he is pretty careful with his work.

Open under Communications because he is outspoken about his opinions.

Group Centric under Motivation because it seems like he wants to serve the company with his service.

Passive under Energy because he only works when instructed.

Assured under Esteem, as he is pretty confident about himself.

Subservience under Compliance because he seems to follow the rules and protocols closely without fail.

His Interaction is Harmonious as he is generally friendly to colleagues.

After we have marked the different qualities, we sum them up under the different Forces, and we get the result that he is Status Quo- 6 and New Order-3. This makes him a Moderate Status Quo person, a normal colleague.

How do we define the traits of the colleagues based on the Qualities of the 9 Opposing Forces? Here is a list:

Status Quo- 8-9 and New Order- 0-1: **Extreme Status Quo.**
Status Quo-6-7 and New Order- 2-3: **Moderate Status Quo.**
Status Quo- 4-5 and New Order- 4-5: **Balanced.**
Status Quo- 2-3 and New Order- 6-7: **Moderate New Order.**
Status Quo- 0-1 and New Order- 8-9: **Extreme New Order.**

Generally, the most challenging colleagues/environment to work with are Extreme New Order by default. However, if you are a Moderate-Extreme New Order types, you may also run into problem with Extreme Status Quo colleagues and environment. The most normal of all colleagues are Moderate Status Quo or Moderate New Order. These people are also the safest that one can encounter, and least likely to give much problems. The most dangerous, surprisingly are the Balanced one. Confused?

Colleagues who fit closer Status Quo are the archetype for order. You can be certain that you are in a company of conscientious folks who do not want disruptions to their work routines, because that will have adverse effects on them on many levels, including their personal well being.

The traits of such co-workers or department are insular, laidback, somewhat cowardly, values work-life balance, are comfortable with familiar processes, non-adventurous and probably see the job as a means to get by till retirement.

These types of workers tend to be found in industries or jobs of the administrative, compliance, and fixed skill sets (e.g. accountancy) nature. It is usually fortunate for like-minded employees to join such organizations, as they can expect a good amount of peacetime and stability. The downside is that you cannot expect much promotions, growth; they tend to act bureaucratic, and when shit hits the fan, these people tend to react extremely selfishly.

On the other hand, those who fit closer to the New Order are the archetype for change. You can be certain that you are in the company of forward thinking folks who are thinking of rewriting a new chapter for the company, who fervently desire to contribute their expertise and know-how to increase efficiency, growth and profit.

The traits of such co-workers are usually dynamic, energetic, somewhat aggressive, values inventiveness and innovations and probably see the job as a means to showcase their ability and to rise in ranks and pays.

These types of workers tend to be found in industries or jobs of the commercial nature. If you are someone who wants opportunities, enterprise, innovations and those things with over the top buzzwords, then you can surely find good company amongst these folks. The downside is that given their go getter nature, they can get combative, competitive, and when shit hits the fan, they are out for your blood.

Most colleagues will fall into Moderate ranges which is acceptable, and the least likely to give you trouble. The two Extremes may be difficult to work with, and are rarer, especially if you have very different values/qualities, but they are rather easy to figure, and frequently fall into easy categorization, like for example, the company villain.

From my experience, the **most dangerous co-workers are incidentally the most 'balanced' ones**, because you cannot clearly define if they are more Status Quo or New Order leaning. Most of the time, they tend to obscure certain aspects of their personality on a rather adept level and may appear ambiguous. These are the colleagues who will also turn out to be highly competent in reading people, concealing their intentions, and having powerful leadership quality, because they can exercise subtle influence in the work environment for not having their minds clouded by extremes. Keep your eyes open and watch out for this type of people.

Identifying
Friends and Foes

This exercise measures the propensity of the colleagues towards 'Friends' and 'Foes'. Of course human interactions are more complex than that; some people simply don't like someone's guts for no obvious reasons, and friends can be made even in the most unlikely circumstances, but here we are testing a likelihood based on tension points between people in the office.

Needless to say, anyone can turn out to be an enemy. The key to dealing with these type of people is to be able to assess who can potentially become one. Most of the time, human beings are equipped with the ability to intuit friendliness and ill-will, but there are times when the other party is hard to read (having balanced traits assessment), or when you are oblivious/mildly autistic to human cues.

The best measure is to take on a simple tension scoring with the table in the next page to assess the other party (or the rest of the colleagues). The basis of this test is based on the situations and positions which the employees are put into, due to company and work arrangements. When people are placed in opposition or at cross purposes, even the best friend on a personal level may be the deadliest enemy at a professional level.

Tension Scoring

Contender	Superior	Giver
5	5	5
4	4	4
3	3	3
2	4	2
1	5	1
Ally	Subordinate	Recipient

Low Range- 5-7
Middle Range- 8-11
High Range- 12-15

The Tension Scoring table is divided into three columns with varying scores at each row within the column. The three columns are namely Contender/Ally, Superior/Subordinate and Giver/Recipient. The scores are ranked from 1-5.

Contender- The colleague who are assessed together with you on the same set of tasks, have overlap in job function, are doing projects that are at opposition/cross purposes with yours, on in your opposing camp in the political game.

Ally- Colleague who is likely to benefit together with you, or on your side in political game.

Superior- Colleague who is higher up in the hierarchy, whom you report to, or you serve (e.g. your boss).

Subordinate- Colleague who is below you, who reports to you or serves you.

Giver- The colleague in a support relationship with you, who provides resources or services for you to get your work done (e.g. IT support guy who help you solve IT issues).

Recipient- Colleague whom you support, whereby you provide resources or services for (e.g. if you are in R&D team, you make products for the product managers).

The scores do not strictly follow any order, but they are based on the scale which you feel the other party likely fall into. The numbers closer to a representation of either type is chosen in each column and added up. True neutral scores are 3 in all columns. After the numbers are added up, we will look at the ranges. Low Range- 5-7 indicates a potentially amicable professional relationship. Middle Range- 8-11 indicates a neutral professional relationship. High Range- 12-15 indicates a potentially testy professional relationship. This is not an indicator on outright friendliness or hostility, but rather a test of potential tension. Tension that is built up at the High Range usually means that the other party will feel like at some point, not too pleased with you.

Example 1: Amy the logistics manager.

You rate her 3 in Contender/Ally because she belongs to another department, with no conflict of interest.

You rate her 4 in Superior/Subordinate because while she does not report to you, her title is lower than yours.

You rate her 5 in Giver/Recipient because you always rely on her for arranging and coordinating shipment.

The overall score is 12, which is on the high range, therefore potentially testy.

Example 2: Jonathan, a salesperson in your team.

You rate him 4 in Contender/Ally because he is a salesperson just like you with the same goals and targets to meet, and will likely be assessed by your boss similarly. He is not given a 5 because his accounts are separate from yours, therefore not in direct competition.

You rate him 3 in Superior/Subordinate because he is at the same level, bearing the same title and the same job responsibility as you.

You rate him 2 in Giver/Recipient because you frequently pass on leads which falls under his accounts to him.

The overall score is 9, is middle range, therefore may lead to a neutral relationship.

There is no guarantee that the individuals with tension scores at the low or middle range will not turn antagonistic at some point in time. We have to understand that given that the workplace dynamics do shift all the time, the tension scores do not remain static.

However, these indicators are a good gauge on existing conditions, and potential allies or foes one will make throughout the course of his or her career. The key to thriving well in office politics is to align with the 'friends' (Low Range scores), influence the neutral co-workers (Middle Range scores), and stay cautious of those 'enemies' (High Range scores), hopefully to be able to convert them over to your side as well.

Identifying the Competitors

It is one thing to be able to survive the office; it is another to be able to thrive well and get ahead. In order to get ahead, whether in terms of attaining a better position in the company, getting a fancier title or having more in the salary, it definitely involves some degree of competition. Of course, not every job is competitive in nature; there are jobs where everyone does the same thing, unlike say sales or other jobs defined by performance. Yet, I presume that most of my readers probably want to get ahead in their job, and by that token, the competition can take place even in the non-competitive jobs.

A competitor or rival is not necessarily someone who openly challenges one in the workplace. Rather, this person is someone who can potentially be a threat to the progress, goals and even job stability of the employee, because this person is poised at a high advantage to get ahead. The friendliest colleague can be a potential rival if he or she has the requisite to do so. Therefore, it is crucial for the employee to identify the rivals from the many colleagues in the company; using prior knowledge from the previous exercises in power and social gauges, character traits and identification of the person whether as a friend, foe or not, to form a good profile of the person; and then to test out the competition scoring test to complete the profiling.

Competition Scoring

Charisma		Influence		Importance		Performance		Likeability (Office)	
Strong	5	Strong	6	Strong	6	Good	8	High	5
Medium	3	Medium	3	Medium	3	Normal	3	Normal	3
Weak	1	Weak	1	Weak	1	Bad	1	Low	1
Likeability (Other Departments)		Likeability (Superiors)		Energy		Style			
High	6	High	8	Active	5	Political	5		
Normal	3	Normal	3	Neutral	3	Neutral	3		
Low	1	Low	1	Passive	1	Apolitical	1		

In the table above, there are 9 columns, made up of Charisma, Influence, Importance, Performance, Likeability (Office), Likeability (Other Departments), Likeability (Superiors), Energy and Style. Each of the column are made up of 3 rows in descending order from a high score, through medium score to a low score. The different indicators are:

Charisma- How much charm the person has. This may not just depend on the outlook, but rather the ability to command interest, good feelings and admiration from people.

Influence- How much influence a person has over other people. One way to find out influence is to see if the other party readily gets affected by the words, action and behavior from the person; usually by paying attention to, obeying to, and reacting to, the person. Most influencer also wields considerable power.

Importance- Whether the person holds important function in the company. It does not necessarily equate to superiority, but whether this function or position is critical for the success of the operations.

Performance- How well the person performs his or her function. The measure of performance can be qualitative (how well the work is done) or quantitative (how much is achieved).

Likeability (Office)- How popular the person is within the office setting.

Likeability (Other Departments)- How the different departments view the person.

Likeability (Superiors)- How popular the person is with the superiors and upper management.

Energy- The attitude towards work and action in general, whether the person does things proactively or not.

Style- Whether the person enjoys politicking in the company or not.

Within each column, select the most likely score, then add up all the scores from the nine columns. If the person gets an overall score between 9-12, this person ranks low in the competition, not a threat at all, and may not even be able to save himself/herself. If the person gets an overall score between 13-27, this person is considered as somewhat mediocre. If the person gets an overall score between 28- 35, this person has the potential to be a worthy competitor. And if the person gets an overall score between 36-54, this person can be a threat to the employee.

Find Out the
Political Factions

Slightly over 2 weeks into the job, the newcomer may learn about the interpersonal dynamics between colleagues, boundaries, potential friends and enemies. Within 2 months into the job, alliances would have been forged (unless you're a loner), and one may get a pretty good sense of the politics in the office. Yet such alliances and notions are still premature, because political factions may be more complex, intricate and sublime. Some of the obvious politicking may turn out to be false flags. And the alliances formed are on a more superficial ground, based on comfort and convenience, and not necessarily based on political affinity.

It is dangerous to misconstrue political dynamics at both individual and group levels, as they can lead to wrong ideas and decisions made; the employee should be patient and cautious when uncovering the intricacy of politics within the office. Political factions are formed according to the different political affinity of the colleagues. Political affinity is driven by necessity than convenience, and is a confluence of contention and ambition. In our previous exercises, we discussed at great lengths about the interactions of five other departments, opposing forces at the workplace, and tension scorings. These are the drivers for contention. On the other hand, personal goals and aspirations, personality, power and social gauges, the competition scorings, hierarchy structures, and admittance to 'Old Boys Club' are the drivers for ambition.

In order to uncover political factions, one should begin by looking out for cues and conflict points. Cues are more literal observations of two parties: how they interact, any perceived hostility and discontent, and if they have even openly admitted their dislikes for the other party during those pantry sessions.

Conflict points are based on rational analysis. Conflict points at the macro level happen frequently at 'Counterparts', and 'Givers/Recipients' relationships across the different departments and job functions, as well as the overarching philosophical forces between 'Status Quo' and 'New Order'. At the next level, try to figure out any tension points between the parties to see if they are on propensity towards friendly or hostile terms. Narrow down to the individuals' competitive advantage by scoring and see where he or she will stand. Normally, individuals with similar competitive standing then to band together, or become mortal nemesis (if they are both high on competitive scores).

Upon identification of cues and conflict points, a preliminary idea of the political factions should be formed. With this information at hand, do continually observe, as political factions themselves can also be dynamic in nature, influenced by circumstances and the fleeting human relationships. At some point, the employee may inevitably get sucked into this whole political game; a topic which we will cover later on in the book.

Face and Body Reading

Physiognomy (reading bodies and faces), in modern days, is frequently underestimated or dismissed as new age (or dated) pseudo-science, but it has been frequently correlated to personality and behavior. Even the FBI employs some degree of such study to analyze people.

This exercise looks at both face and body reading. They are based primarily on my personal observations and findings and while there are certain propensity towards the correlations between the forms and the behaviour/personalities, we have to understand that correlation does not always equal causation. A person with eyes typified as those shapes belonging to villains may not turn out to be a villain. Although the probability is high. Therefore, I would encourage the readers to exercise discretion and judgement; hear what I have got to say here, agree or agree to disagree, and form your conclusions.

a) **Face Shape**- Through my years of observations, I came across an interesting correlation between major asshole behaviour and those people with square (and somewhat protruding) jawlines.

Usually, there are not much dramas amongst junior staffs with these features, but once the hyper virile jawlines are found on the faces of senior managers and executives, there is a likelihood to expect three major jerk moves: bullying, fingerpointing and backstabbing.

I suspect that these people have a tendency to be slightly sociopathic, vindictive, and probably enjoy inflicting "psychological torture" on the co-workers.

If the colleague with the square jawlines is lean and have a somewhat angular and skinny face and narrow eyes, this person may turn out to be Norman Bates in the making. If the person with such jawline takes a rotund form, chances are this person is rude, obnoxious and quite "base".

On separate notes, I also have found many employees with rounder face (especially males) will tend to act manipulative and cowardly, especially if they have attractive eyes. The person with an inverted triangle face (big forehead, narrow chin) are usually clever, introverted and calculating.

The person with narrow face (skull compressed from both sides and tapered like a bird) tend to be difficult and pushy. Those with big face is usually unscrupulous and love playing dirty. But the worst of the worst always seems to be the chads with the defining square jaws.

b) **Eyes**- The eyes are the windows to the soul, or so they say; but the results are usually deceptively different from what conventional face-readings teach you. In my interactions, the most dangerous kind of people are those with conventionally beautiful, attractive eyes.

The beautiful, attractive eyes can take on any color, but they usually exude a potent mix of allure and innocence, with a watery quality. The problem with this type of people is that while you are charmed off your pants, they can potentially take you down off guard. Colleagues with this quality are usually charming, diplomatic, insincere, manipulative but will set you up for surprises when things turn south.

Let's move on and talk about the obviously sinister types. 'Sanpaku', a Japanese word, describes sclera (white) surrounding the iris from three sides. There are the yin sanpaku type and the yang sanpaku type. The yin type has the whites showing on the left, right and the bottom of the iris. People with these features are usually reckless, and often attract mishaps and accidents.

The yang type, with whites on left, right and top of iris are the dangerous ones you should look out for. Co-workers with these eyes often have cruel and sadistic qualities, and are usually dangerous when crossed. Search up Hilary Clinton and Jimmy Savile as the poster-boys for this type of eyes.

On the other sinister types, there are those with beady eyes- I view them as aggressive opportunists with penchant for office politics. And last but not least, the 'Triangular' eyes, literally eyes shaped like right angled scalar triangles. I noticed that there is a correlation with these eyes and amoral behavior, whereby the person is willing to do anything to achieve their goals.

c) **Ears**- Ears can often inform about a person's character. Whenever I see a person with ears that are distinctively small on a face, I'd usually try to find out if they can be challenging to work with (and yes they are). If a person has long attached earlobe (that means no distinct earlobes that stick out) that sticks to the side of the face, there is a chance that this person is highly argumentative. If the earlobes are detached and fat, chances are the person is a rather fair minded person. A person with anti-helix of the ear that curve outward or has ears that look like bat's ears, are often highly rebellious in nature but also creative thinkers.

d) **Nose**- Noses are a gauge of a person's attitude towards money and material comfort. I find noses that look big and bulbous belong to people who are materialistic and also with tendency to act extravagant. Whereas people with noses that are sharp and bony seemed to me mean spirited, petty and calculative.

e) **Fingers**- Fingers inform a person's mindedness and proficiency. A person with short stumpy fingers tend to be stoic, pragmatic and stuck in a rut. Those with medium length fingers are usually in leadership positions, and have the ability to translate ideas into actions. If your bosses have unusually long fingers, they tend to be more cerebral and idealistic, and may not be too good with the practical aspects of things.

f) **Lips and Teeth**- These parts on the face often inform me about the trustworthiness of the person. A person whose smile shows gum is usually forthcoming but can't keep a secret. Those with maxillary prognathism (protruding upper teeth) likes to gossip. People with mouth that hangs slightly ajar and beady eyes are untrustworthy and prone to connivance. A fair faced male who perpetually wears soft smiles are heartless backstabbers. The last two types will use information to their advantage to get back at people. If you have bosses who look like any of the above, do not share your intimate details unless you deliberately want to spread misinformation.

g) **Body Shape and Size**- I have observed that men who are obese, lumpy and slightly awkward (not the spritely agile plump ones, but the sluggish ones) tend to be more easygoing. It may have something to do with decreased testosterone level especially when they are in the middle age. The only problem with this kind of worker is that they tend to be somewhat careless, weak and not really giving their best at work. If you have such a boss, there is a likelihood that he (yes usually males) may not maintain power for long and usually has not much control over subordinates and situations.

Women on the other hand who are relatively plump tend to be someone concerned with security and status quo, and if she doesn't have a partner (and especially if she is big and tall as well), she may behave matronly. Both men and women who are lean and fit tend to be better work performers, but they also tend to be on top of their game. Colleagues who are plus sized once again (big or tall), tend to be easy going, whereas the smaller ones (especially men) may have Napoleon-like qualities: aggressive, perfectionist, demanding, and obsessive compulsive. But highly competent.

h) **Postures and Styles**- What are some of the strange qualities that nice colleagues possess? Look out for people who walk like a duck, literally. Walking like a duck means that their feet are faced outward instead of forward, and people with this quality are usually compassionate, easygoing, and lenient, although they can be a bit of a braggart and can get defensive.

Another strange quality that nice colleagues would likely features is if they are tall and slightly hunched. I find them lenient and easy on their staff if they turn out to be bosses. But do take note, this has to be distinguished from shorter people who are hunched; I have discovered many times throughout my career that the latter type can be potentially malicious and conniving.

3. The Art of Concealment

True power is not easily discerned, otherwise it is not true power. If anyone can see through a person, then that person has lost his or her power. When someone seems intelligent, that person is likely to be not that intelligent. One who wears one's heart on the sleeve will only suffer many heartbreaks. One who frequently speaks his or her mind will not stay long in the job.

Everyone above are big moving targets ready to be pounced upon by predators and detractors, whether in the office or not. The problem is that they do not understand the Art of Concealment. It is one of the most important rules in human interactions, especially if a person is going to be bound in a dangerous place like the office for a period of time, a place festering with all manner of wicked life-forms.

A person who appears too perfect will surely be envied and hated. A person who appears too flawed will surely be despised and discarded. In the office, people are not just concerned with doing the job right and getting paycheck at the end of the month. There will be a significant number of them wanting to get more money and higher status in the company;

and in order to do so, someone has to suffer injustice and to be put down. When a person can be read like a book, that person is the easiest to be manipulated, exploited, and eventually eradicated.

Rather, be like the still water that runs deep, the Lake Placid, where the calmness and serenity on the surface belies the powerful (dangerous) force beneath. If you are brilliant like the luminaries in the sky, then learn to hide the brilliance, until the time is right to blaze all the contenders with the supernova. If you are someone with meagre qualities or is a dysfunctional wretch, cloak those defects away from the prying eyes of predators and start improving your life in secrecy, while acting like a regular functional person. When the time is right, your "miserable past" can be used to amplify the narratives of your successes.

The Art of Concealment essentially, as the name implies, is all about discretions: hiding and concealing. It can range from the physical (downplaying your physical attributes, material possessions in the office), to verbal (holding back your opinions, learning when to shut up) and even ideas/impressions (hiding the fact that you are more ambitious than you look, creating impressions that you are just like everyone else in office).

Hide Your Shine
Especially if you are
New to a Company

Do you sometimes feel that despite the positive qualities that you have and bring to work, you are still put down very often by your boss and your colleagues? If you do, then it is time to start examining the cause of it. First question to ask yourself: have you been following the wrong approach all along? If you are an effective, confident worker who deliver results, but often get passed for promotion, you might have possibly transgressed upon the most critical taboo of all office politics: "The Shine".

Many self-improvement books out there in the market encourage self empowerment: to appear competent, confident and even assertive. These values can surely come in handy and useful at some point in the career, but when a person newly joins a work environment or office, it is not the appropriate thing to do.

Most of the workers in work environment by default (with at least 1 year of establishment of the office employees) are apprehensive of new colleagues, even if that person is supposed to be a welcomed addition to the team. Whenever a new face is added to the department, he/she will usually be judged critically for the appearance, mannerisms, attitude, personality, and work performance, and usually these judgements tend to be personal and subjective. And the first person to judge a new employee is usually the boss himself/herself.

1) Never Outshine the Master

The above title is from Rule No.1 in Robert Greene's excellent book "48 Laws of Power". There must be a reason why it is listed as rule number one in the book, and I suspect that it could have possibly contributed to the highest number of body counts when the rule is transgressed upon.

This first rule from Robert Greene mentions, *"Always make those above you feel comfortably superior. In your desire to please or impress them, do not go too far in displaying your talents or you might accomplish the opposite – inspire fear and insecurity. Make your masters appear more brilliant than they are and you will attain the heights of power."*

The quote essentially sums up the whole meaning of the law, but we could examine it in detail. Let's first look at the boss (as in your immediate superior; the one person whom you report to, who signs your paycheck). He or she is usually also an employee just like yourself, with other bosses to report to, unless he or she is the proprietor or CEO.

The reason why you are hired to work under this boss is because: you are needed to fulfil certain functions that were originally lacking because the functions are either newly created, or you are somebody's replacement.

You may be directly hired by this person you are reporting to, because this person identified that you could help to fulfil the function, or you may be hired by someone else of higher power to work under this boss (and usually in such case, there are higher resistance against you).

The immediate boss would really hope that you: don't give trouble, finish assigned work on time, and stay far away from his or her boss.

When you fulfil your functions, it is supposed to make your immediate boss looks good, so that it becomes a reflection of his or her leadership quality. But at this point you must try to find out the "boundaries", on how much you can do under this boss.

This boss is usually more forgiving or comfortable with you, if he or she sees that you are trying your best to complete the functions (as in putting up a display of struggles e.g. long work hours) and also respecting his or her authority (by consulting, or being somewhat "helpless" with the boss, so that their opinions and advice really matter). However, if you make your work seems rather effortless, or manage to impress the "boss of your immediate boss" with the knowledge of your immediate boss, then you are in some trouble. Your immediate boss will get insecure and may plan to make life difficult for you.

When you, on the other hand becomes obviously superior: showing better looks, results and proficiency than your boss, taking credits and stealing thunder from your boss (can happen quite often in meetings with something as innocuous as the employee giving better oratorical presentations, when compared side by side with the boss), and worse, being popularly deemed as better than the boss, or obviously favored by the "boss of the boss", then you are in big trouble. Your immediate boss will see you as a thorn in the flesh and would try to get you eradicated as soon as possible.

The rule "Never Outshine the Master" therefore needs to be paid with special attention; but there is a strategic extension from this law. Do not seek to impress the "immediate boss" as the latter is usually not impressed , but rather, start to strategize subtle ways to "impress the boss of the boss", without turning it into a suicidal endeavor of greater transgression. This will be expanded upon elsewhere in the book.

2) Don't get Shiny Forehead

There is the boss, and then there are your other colleagues. If you have co-workers reporting to the same boss, and doing comparatively similar functions as you are, then that will be the next group of people that you have to be very careful with. The boss does not like you to "outshine", but your co-workers do not like you to "shine" at all.

When you have a "Shiny Forehead" (that means appearing confident, competent and smug about it) especially in the earlier periods of you working in the new work environment, you will be marked down almost immediately by both your boss and your peers. Your immediate boss may be obliged to praise you, but you will be quick to attract envy and insecurities from all fronts.

There is really no use to give "Shiny Forehead" that early in any office work, because it does not guarantee you any tangible success and longevity for your career.

When you deliver too much in the beginning, you are bound to wane later.

When you first join a company, and deliver good results too fast, your co-workers will prepare your doomsday clock in the hope for your quick and imminent downfall. When you are burnt out or fail to deliver at some point, you will then be labelled as big time loser and judged more critically than the usual poor performer.

Always try to gauge the performances of your colleagues and align yourself to similar levels, even if it means downplaying of your potential.

What I mean by downplaying of your potential is not to be a poor performer deliberately, but rather to "hold your horses", if you are generally a highly proficient worker. This lowers the guard of your colleagues, allowing you time to understand them better (strengths, weaknesses, motivations, alignment), to safeguard from potential sabotage, and allowing you to quietly build your base, gather resources, and plan your "epic moment of launch" (discussed further in the book).

3) No Shiny Diamonds

Do you wear expensive clothes, is exceptionally good looking, drives a bigger and more expensive car than your boss, wears large diamond rings or came from elite school of top standings? If you have any of these, you must learn to downplay those qualities, in front of your bosses and colleagues. No one likes show offs, and people get jealous not just from performances, but also by your appearances and perceived successes.

The sad reality of the office is that it is largely made up of people who are dissatisfied with their current state of life. If people are in the working class, then there are high chances that they frequently put up with many struggles in their lives. They likely have mortgages or student loans to pay up, am worried about taking care of their ailing parents and/or making the best for their kids at school, have growing health concerns and also insecurity about their financial and career status and stability by their mid '30s, and is bleeding financially from all these commitments. And more often than not, when they see the privileged few, they will almost instantly harbor resentments, envy and even utter contempt.

If you are truly loaded, technically you should not even be working for other people at all. But if you are a working class person and has the extra money to splurge on and buy expensive cars and big diamond rings, you will always be singled out by the rest of the working class as a bourgeois with that extra dollars and condemned.

Therefore, if you are not rich enough to be not working in the offices, do not try to impress with your little bit of wealth. If you are already blessed with good looks, dressing down (not sloppy; refer to topic on dressing in the book) or downplaying other qualities is a smart move. If you are an Ivy league scholar, just keep the smarts inside, as there is no need to impress regular working folks with normal IQ; they won't get it.

Hide Your Quirks

There is a Japanese proverb, "Nails that sticks out gets hammered down". This saying makes a point that when a person is deemed as different or deviant, he or she is met with resistance. We all know that the Japanese society is one of conformity and homogeneity, where everybody is expected to think, act and look the same way. However, this is not a unique cultural phenomena. It is also the same in every work place, even in the Western world.

If you are conscious you are the type that is different from convention, then be very mindful of the effect it can bring. It is safe to appear different outside of work. But when it comes to the office, it bears a dangerous social stigma.

Do not draw attention to your "different" personality and/or try to distinguish oneself from the rest of the colleagues, as the "unique" one; this is the most unwise thing to do. But if you naturally already come across as different, then try to hide it if possible, and blend in with the crowd in the office. We all know that odd person in the office. And the unfortunate thing is that this odd person is usually left out, dines alone, teased at, and gets bullied at work.

The office is generally a place of conformity. Uniforms (office attires are also uniforms) are worn for uniformity. The work-tie is a reminder of slavery. The "Core" values of the company are enforced codes for employees to abide to, and carry out. Therefore the company often expects employees to behave, look and think the same way, performance (of course the most important part) aside.

If you are already different or have strange quirky thoughts, you must learn to camouflage it and also keep opinions to yourself. Most of your colleagues do not appreciate quirky or "special people" (unless you are in the "arts" type of work environment). The "regular" office folks prefer to be in the company of their own kind, which is usually mediocre, boring, and they tend to talk inane shit (kids, holidays). They will look at the person funny if the person brings up Dostoyevsky.

If you look, act and speak differently, they will presume that you also think differently from them, and feel you are threatening the values they hold dear, and therefore they will do their best to ostracize you, ridicule you and worse, turn you into the perfect effigy and convenient scapegoat.

Sometimes a quirky soul may find company in similar counterpart, and quick friendship are surely formed, but unless that other person is the boss, chances are it will be a scenario of two ostracized workers in the office.

Maintaining Personal Privacy
And Keeping Opinions to Yourself

This goes beyond the "Do not wash your dirty linen in public" idiom. It is not wise at all to discuss about what you do in your private life or what your private opinions are like, especially when it is embarrassing, controversial and/or anything that reflects badly on your image.

But it is not even necessary for anyone to know too much about your private life even if it is not embarrassing or controversial. Conceal you must, your true personality and thoughts, and also details of your private life.

This maintenance of personal privacy is not merely a protection on your reputation, but also a strategy to keep antagonists at bay. Yet while we need to maintain personal privacy, we cannot be too rigid with this, as it will surely raise suspicion and distrust. If you're a young adult, you will often be asked questions about which schools you came from and whether you have any girlfriend/boyfriend. If you're an adult, you will be asked questions about how many kids you have. These are questions that other colleagues will enquire when a person newly joins a company, and they should be answered truthfully, because the truth will eventually reveal itself and if your accounts change at some point down the road, you are going to sound suspicious and appear distrustful. As a rule of thumb, unless asked, there is no point in telling people anything about your personal affairs.

At lunch breaks, all kinds of things can be discussed, but there are certain things that should never be brought up. Below are what I define as personal matters and opinions to be more discrete about:

1. **Your previous relationship with your colleagues in your previous jobs (especially if it is not a pleasant one).** Comments about former company or colleagues need to be positive even if it is not the case, or best not to mention at all. Because all ears are on potential words that can be used against you, as well as getting a sense of your personality, and even moral values. Never ever talk badly about former companies or colleagues in front of your current colleagues. Because if you can do something like that, they will think you can do it to the current company and colleagues.

2. **Do not wash your dirty linen in public (reprise).** Sometimes when a person gains trust with other colleagues in the office, they became less discrete and gave more details about their personal affairs like: complaining about their kids not doing well in school, their quarrels with spouses, their personal mental struggles/depressions, or even their deviant habits. These are strictly not to be mentioned, as they are easy to remember, and again can be used as words/evidence against you.

Never ever talk private affairs to colleagues especially if they do not reflect well on yourself, your family members and/or loved ones. Talking badly about your family members, will make you look especially bad.

3. **Your political, racial, sexual and religious inclinations.** It is acceptable for people to know what religious group you belong to, unless it is an unorthodox religion or cult, then you have to keep it a secret. But since the company is likely to be a secular environment, one should not discuss freely about belief systems. Understandably, different States bear different political sentiments and it can be reflected in the company where you are situated in.

   However, in most MNCs (Multi-National Corporations), its superficial image is always slightly left leaning. They will pretend to value things like racial equality, female empowerment, gender equality. If you ever do transgress on any of these, you are in big trouble as they can be used as effective weapons with almost immediate effects of dismissal or career end, if they do get to the HR.

4. **Do not have displays of affection, success and happiness in the workplace.** I have mentioned before that when a person appears too perfect, he or she is bound to be envied upon and hated. Here, we are not even talking about work performance or skill-sets, but rather on personal life.

Let's start with the greatest pet peeves in the normal office. It is surprisingly "loving relationships", more so than financial status. In the office, there are bound to be several co-workers (especially single women) who are dissatisfied with their relationships. Mind you, there are also dissatisfied parents, spouses, and the list goes on. If you've announced how awesome the new girlfriend/boyfriend is to you, how great your kids are, how loving you have relationships with your parents, or spouses, or kids, there is a good chance that it will bring about the displeasure of some green-eyed monsters in the midst. As a rule of thumb, don't share such personal joys to the office, it will only attract envy and contempt.

Besides not announcing your "loving relationships" to the office, also take note not to put up photos of your family, spouse, kids in the office. There is a common misconception that showing the pictures will depict how positive or regular one is. But these pictures can stir jealousy and resentment from co-workers who struggle with relationships or have dysfunctional family.

5. **Do not disclose personal information.** This can vary from the schools you came from, the range of salary you drew, your address, your ID number or even your birthday. While it is understandable that addresses, salary amount and ID numbers are way too sensitive information, one might ask why do I even raise the alarm on something as innocuous as what school a person came from or his/her birthday?

Well, these information are actually not much different from the range of salary, ID number or address, because these are also information that can profile a person. There are only so much an employee can show in the office; physical attributes, the way they speak, and the quality of their work. But through gathering of such sensitive information, a person can be effectively profiled more holistically than ever before. Something like which schools a person came from can speak volume about his/her educational, family and even financial background. Something as innocent as the birthday can get this person to be typecast into certain personality (traits and weaknesses are shown) based on astrological profiling.

When someone asks for your birth dates down to the birth time, that person is usually up to no good! It may not be just casual astrology profiling, as it can even extend into hex and sorcery by the more superstitiously inclined.

6. **Be careful of gossips!** Gossip about other colleagues, your bosses, your company may be enjoyed by almost everybody, but at the expense of the talker, because it creates a bad impression of the person, automatically lowering the trust index of the person. Because if someone can gossip to a person about something, there is a good chance that he or she can also gossip about this person to other people.

Reserve Comments About Co-workers

Let's say Jane finds out from someone that another colleague of hers, Adam, had been commenting about her work attitude. The comment mentioned Jane as 'hardworking'. How do you think Jane will feel about this supposedly 'positive' comment? She will probably not take it positively; she may think that Adam was trying to imply that she is not so clever, so therefore she has to work hard, although this comment could have originated from a good place.

We can see that when a colleague passes any comment about another colleague, there is a good chance that it will be received and perceived with a certain amount of suspicion, doubt, and imagined ill will, because human beings tend to overthink. When an employee is in a complex environment like the office, it is best to mind one's own business and not to pass comments about any person in the office.

Because words will surely spread- propagated by the office gossip and the original message tend to get distorted as they are passed on (potentially turning an originally innocuous comment like "Jane is hardworking" to something like "Jane has worked too hard"). By keeping opinions to yourself and not making comments about co-workers, you can save yourself from potential misunderstandings, troubles and even political enmity.

Conceal Your Intentions

There are no thought police to catch us for our intentions. Yet, sometimes through certain words, actions and behavior, are our intentions accidentally revealed to the other party. When such things happen in the office, even if most of the colleagues don't get it, when you have one or two perceptive colleagues who are sharp enough to pick it up, that will be enough to expose your thoughts.

Be careful of the words, actions and the way you carry yourself, the subtle cues which give away your secret intentions.

One of the greatest mistakes that anyone can commit in the office is with the revealing of career ambitions. Especially to your boss.

You might recall that when you first went for the interviews, the interviewer or hirer may sometimes ask questions like, "what do you want to achieve in 5 years time in the company", "what are your career ambitions".

Those are baits for entrapment; precarious moments in the interview, especially if the interviewer is going to be your direct boss. The most politically correct way to answer such questions is something along the line of wanting to contribute a lot to the company in the next 5 years, and improving on doing the SAME job which you applied for. In effect, you should plant the idea in their heads that you are willing to be the "Perfect Slave", even though you are not. This will relax their guard, trust you better and if you do get the job, will likely have an easier time with the boss.

Your career ambitions if you have any, obviously are detrimental to your boss if he or she doesn't get promoted along with you. For you to climb onto the next level, you are effectively taking your bosses' level. Never ever share the career ambitions and aspirations to your direct bosses, as well as your other colleagues, and very importantly: your subordinates if you have any.

Your co-workers all pray that you will not go far, because they are also vying for the same thing, unless they are disinterested slobs. If you have any subordinates, they are the people who hope to precipitate your downfall so they can get a levelling chance and they will most certainly carry tales to other colleagues and even your boss.

Aside from ambitions and aspirations; it you have plans to execute your work in a certain way that goes under the radar, then very well maintain it under the radar, especially if it has some malicious intent. Do not share your secret plans with anybody, but yourself.

Hide Your Weaknesses

We are all imperfect in some ways but we should never make a show of it. Most employees do not want to be seen as the weakest link in the organization. People who appear too perfect are often hated, but people who appear too weak are also despised. In any work organization, a person who is seen as weak or inefficient are deemed useless and has a high chance of getting fired/replaced.

If you have apparent weaknesses, learn to hide it, without overcompensation. For example, if you are bad in talking, then talk less, rather than talk more (talking less sometimes even create an illusion of respectability). Outside of work, learn to improve on your talking skills so you can unleash your improvement at the most opportune time. If you have internal weaknesses, do not confide with anybody in the office, because chances are it will spread throughout the whole office. Know and improve your weaknesses, but never admit them.

There is actually a reverse to this rule which can be used which I talked about in "Display Minor Weaknesses" in under the chapter "Projecting the Right Image". This is about showing acceptable weaknesses as part of a professional persona. The whole point is to hide away real weaknesses while creating a façade of imperfection with minor weaknesses which will not reduce the professional image.

Control Your Emotions

When an employee is in the company of people, any 'interesting' emotional display will immediately garner the attention of the co-workers. Because strong emotional displays are great drama for otherwise another uneventful day in the office, rousing keen interest from the sleepy employees and they will be easily remembered, and used as conversation pieces for a long time.

The most 'interesting' emotional displays tend to be negative ones; projections of anger and sadness, because these displays are rarer, or rather unexpected from a professional setting like the office.

On a more uneventful scale, anxiety and stress are probably not as 'interesting', but they serve as convenient labels and 'punchlines' for the bored colleagues. To save oneself from unnecessary attention and judgement, the wise employee should constantly keep emotions in check, and not let them emerge during trying times. The human being is capable of a wide range of emotions, but the ones below are commonplace at work.

1. Curb Your Enthusiasm

"Wise men say only fools rush in..." You may be eager to prove your worth, or may have chanced upon a potentially enriching opportunity at work. But if you are the harried person who hurries through schedule eagerly, you may be deemed an eager beaver, than an idol of admiration by your co-workers. Because the one who is on fire may not just get burnt out, he or she may also turn into a spectacle. We frequently see advertisements and memes based on a famous quote from motivational posters produced by the British government from 1939, 'Keep Calm and Carry On'. This is fashionable, especially in the new millennium, whereby calm, composed attitude and prevalence of cool logic over hot emotionality is perceived as epitome of cool. The over eager individual is simply deemed uncool.

It is universally taught that one should appear calm in most work situation, even though you may not feel like it. The eager beaver may not win fans, because people are programmed to be impressed by efforts that seemed effortless, than a display of enthusiasm and hard work, even though the results may be the same for the two approaches.

But! When we rationalize this enough, it may not be the most appropriate strategy to always appear cool and calm. When we look at the desired effects, we have to break it down to the target audience.

You can actually appear 'slightly harried' in the presence of your immediate boss, and immediate colleagues. This is a strategy to inform them that you are actually working hard, and care enough for the assignments, that you are also a mortal being just like them. Do not be 'too harried' though, because you will turn out to look incompetent instead. On the other hand, if you have any opportunity to do so, try to make your work seem absolutely effortless to the boss of your boss, or to the top dogs in the upper management. They may be the right audience who are suitably impressed.

2. The Stress Face

The enthusiastic eager beaver is better at any time of the day than the stress face. One can appear slightly harried without much attention, but to look stressed out, that is an ultimate no-go zone that will condemn the employee into a certain judgement. The stress face tends to be judged very harshly; he or she may be automatically regarded as incompetent, a greenhorn, has lack of experience and fortitude, or have certain weaknesses in character.

We always have to be mindful of one thing: a person's capability is not entirely based on performance in the company, he or she is also judged on how crisis is managed and work is handled; and the display of stress, which encompasses aspects like lack of confidence or astuteness, heightened anxiety and frustrations, impatience and negativity that may be manifested, is seen as a very lousy sign on any employee.

The stress face tends to be a favourite target amongst detractors. They are usually teased at by co-workers ("hey chillax buddy!"), and sometimes can lead to taunting, condescension and ostracization. Therefore, one should be mindful to NOT APPEAR in this mode, even if one can't help feeling the dread and anxiety building up within. Of course, it may not turn out to be easy to assume a calm demeanor, to put on a poker face and to hide away the stress, when a person is triggered by strong emotional stimulus related to work, especially if the person is predisposed to anxiety.

One way to mitigate this difficulty is to reduce appearances in front of the rest of the colleagues. Minimize contact by writing emails instead of having conversations. And if encounter is imminent, look for ways to mask the dread written on the face, by claiming physically sick, diverting stress reasons away from work cause (telling your colleagues that something unfortunate had happened in your personal life; they tend to be more forgiving of that than to find out that work is the cause of the stress), and even better, to immerse oneself in cheerful situations to make one momentarily forget about the stress.

3. Anger Management

What is way more dangerous than a stress face at the office? Outburst of anger. This should never take place under all circumstances, in any situation. I had seen how this precisely costed jobs of my ex-colleagues in the past. In many organizations, displays of anger like threats, cussings, shouts, and aggressions are tantamount to harassment, and are dealt with very seriously. The worst types are when things get physical; that is immediately criminal. The human resources department actively try to clamp down on such behavior, the least are warnings and black marks and the more severe practice can lead to termination or even lawsuits.

Regardless of whether the employee or the other party is fundamentally right or wrong in their disagreements, the aggressor is usually deemed wrong almost immediately if he or she is the first to show the outburst of anger or physical action.

The hothead who made an outburst of anger will not just be perceived as a bad tempered person; he or she is also judged as having little self control, obnoxious, unprofessional, have severe character flaws and even as stupid (because intelligent people are understood to have a good control over emotions). The receiving end will almost immediately dislike the person, and will probably be thinking of legit and 'professional' ways to do the person in, usually through complaints made to the management, or the HR. The commotion would have probably attracted the attention of third party that are not involved (other colleagues), and these incidences may tarnish the reputation of the aggressor, as words will surely get around in the offices. The wise employee should constantly keep their emotions in check, particularly when they feel angry or slighted, over any likely injustice, disagreement, or discontent. If a person is predisposed to anger, it is imperative not to make a display of it in any professional setting.

Do Not Show Grievances

Sooner than later, the average employee will feel dissatisfied or unhappy at work. Perhaps the work may not live up to expectations, gets too challenging or unrewarding, or colleagues are problematic. There are always much to complain about, but we should be mindful to not show such grievances.

Complaints, more often than not, somehow subconsciously imply that the person is using 'excuses' and justifications for incompetency, reflecting badly on the complainer. The average person may not realize it, but these effects somehow inform the brain of the other party of such an impression.

If not done frequently, the occasional complaints are temporary comedic reliefs that come out from the cubicles, and may not be regarded much, especially when it is trivial and not serious. But if the complaints are made frequently, or sounds serious and/or threatening, bad impressions of the complainer are usually formed.

The immediate boss generally does not like to hear complaints. If the complaints are about political rivals or general bitchy gossip, they may sometimes be entertained, but if they pertain to work or the job function, it may make the boss gets rather annoyed with the subordinate. When it comes to work, most bosses like to hear good news and outcome about the employees' job functions, because it somehow improves the standing of his or her team, improves chances of hitting targets, as well as affirmation of his or her leadership. But complaints and statements of failures are annoyances which actually reduce the person's standing in the eyes of the boss, creating doubts about the person's capability. Therefore, one should be very careful not to vent those grievances onto the boss.

Likewise, complaints may in turn be used as a political weapon by the antagonists, especially if they are severe and have certain controversial or anti-company subtext. Spoken words are difficult to capture as evidence unless recorded.

However, if there is a crowd, there can be several witnesses who can confirm on the authenticity of the complaints. Therefore, one should also be careful not to vent those grievances in the office, especially where there's a group of people.

Do Not Be Caught Skiving

The last thing that a company wants is to regret the decision of hiring a person who is not helpful. There is actually nothing wrong with being lazy; it is one of those great catalysts for innovations. But being lazy is one of the least appreciated traits of employees in the company, because a company wants value for money.

If possible, they really hope to get an absolute slave who can work 24/7 if not for regulations and worker's rights. There are of course some lazy people who can get away with being lazy, especially if they have performances or results which make the company depend on them; but laziness is mostly frowned upon.

Even if laziness is in your blood, try not to look like you are lazy. Do not ever be caught skiving by anyone in the office, even by the friendliest and most trusted ally, because it is certainly something that can be spread around and bitched about. The first person who will give the most attention to this is the immediate boss; they may be lazy themselves, but they do not like their reputation to be tainted by a lazy staff (who may potentially blow their cover if investigated), or they might even identify this employee as the weakest link to be used for their own disposal- a scapegoat to dump all the problems at.

Be A Cautious Change Agent

We understood in 'Opposing Forces in the Workplace' that there are primarily 2 forces in opposition, namely the Status Quo and the New Order. A company over time will tend to display characteristics of one dominant forces, and in majority of the organizations, the Status Quo force usually prevail.

When a person first joins a company, he or she may be observed and assessed on whether his or her values can gel well with the dominant force in the office. Even in the most dynamic organization with a strong New Order characteristic, also do not like an incoming employee to affect and change the way they work and do things.

There are times, unfortunately, when a person is hired exactly for this purpose: to be a change agent. This sort of scenario happens often in restructuring and/or merger, whereby the infusion of new blood is to affect change.

When this happens, expect plenty of resistances from the team, who will not be too happy when someone intend to upset the so-called 'status quo'.

If you are a change agent, always take time to effectuate change in a gradual manner, otherwise if one is limited by time constraints to do so, then one may have to see whether the influencer has any power over the target; to see if it is possible to enforce changes as a process of a certain higher management mandate.

If you are not an assigned change agent, but merely an employee with better ideas and implementation, then you might have to keep them up your sleeves, and learn to adapt and blend into the majority community within the office, especially when one is not of sufficient power to push changes. This will save you many troubles, altercations and even political opponents in the new environment which you are joining.

Feigning Ignorance

For any person who knows too much, especially about information that cannot be known to him or her, he or she may run the risk of getting into problem if found out. Ignorance is bliss, and truths may be hard to handle sometimes, but as with our discussions in 'Propriety and Knowledge', it is always good to know more. The only difference is that there is no need to share this knowledge or claim to have this knowledge.

In the company, especially when it gets large and complex; there are certain things that are out of sight for the normal eyes, and forbidden for the prying minds. Be it insider information, undisclosed news, insidious political plays at work, or even something as simple as someone else's salary information. When the employee knows too much about things that are not supposed to be known, this employee is definitely held as a threat and is at the company's disposal to 'handle' them appropriately when found out. If it is already known, do not mention it, and feign ignorance when asked.

There are also information which are less secretive and dangerous- it can be about an employee who knows his or her work too well, and possibly at risk of transgressing the rules of "Outshining the Master". To make sure it doesn't happen, learn well to hide the shine and not show the cards, as with most rules under "The Art of Concealment".

Time Your Performance

Or do not deliver too much at the beginning. You may be talented, have many ideas, and is a proficient worker. However, what good it does to make a show of these too early in the job? Why not hide it until the time is right?

The supernova explodes in a blinding light show before fizzling into a black hole. The trailblazer burns intensely, too much, too fast; and gets burnt out, running out of gas prematurely on the job highway.

You wouldn't want to be in that situation, unless you are choreographing a momentous epic exit out of the company. When you begin in a job, and you commit too much in the beginning, you may not have the stamina to continue. When you show all your cards in the beginning, you have no trump card to show hand at the end. It is not just harmful to your health; it is also bad for your reputation, because people would then see you as a 3 minutes wonder.

Let's look at some scenarios for you to ponder on. a) Richard regularly turned up early at work and showed enthusiasm for the first month. By the second month, he started to turn up late and shows lack of interest. b) Jane gave so many marketing ideas in the first meeting. She ran out of ideas subsequently. c) Darren closed many deals in the first year; in the following year he did not even clinch a single deal in the entire year. You should get the drift and avoid all the aforementioned situations.

What you can do; if you want to remain in the job for a good amount of time, do conserve your energy, and pace/time yourself. It is OK to not give impressive results earlier in the job, because you are not expected to fly before you take baby steps (unless you are hired as a miracle worker).

If you have good plans and ideas, hide them up your sleeves, and use them judicially in a discerning manner; release them slowly at appropriate timing. If you have certain periods of dearth in performance, subsequent improvement is usually viewed more favorably; compared to 3 minutes wonders who can get propelled into the halls of shame.

Be Careful with Information Technology

Think twice before you surf the internet next time, with your company's network. It is perhaps a little known secret, but the Information Technology (IT) team in the company can easily trace activities on your personal computer on its network, especially if the device is provided by the team.

The other marvels of the IT is that they can also trace your movement if you are issued mobile devices from them.

Of course many people could get away with it, but it is not because the IT is unable to do so, but more likely that it doesn't warrant them to deep dive into each and every persons' details, unless the company perceives the person as a threat.

There are certain things which may be flagged on the company's network, ranging from the obviously bad (games, porn), to questionable (social media, news), and to things which will put them on alert (job hunting sites, communications with competitors). When an employee is handled any devices by the company, they should be immediately regarded as unsafe, and to be treated with extra caution.

There are many ways to track an employee, and as a safety measure, do not surf unnecessarily on those devices, unless it's related to work, do not gossip about someone in the company on the corporate issued social communicators, and do always keep the webcam on the laptop covered.

Another thing is with regards to the handling of information. When even sometimes the casual surfing can be deemed harmless, a definite no-go is to transfer any company information out of the device. There should be company-approved cloud storage or other places where the employee can store information at, but one should be extra cautious if the information is transferred into thumb-drives, or into personal cloud storage. Such acts could even constitute certain breach of security and/or information, and can be tantamount to legal actions.

Hide Your Work Information And Mask Work Progress

While most of your colleagues won't take interest in your work, it is still prudent to keep them protected and hidden away, because there is bound to be someone who will. Those who might take interest are likely not doing so for the best intent to the employee, because there is a high chance that the motive is competitive, malicious or plagiaristic. On a separate note, the employee would have at times, been required to show what they have been up to, either during meetings or via reports to the bosses.

However, those information that are shared should not be the entirety of what is available to the employee, because to show all the cards is just plain foolish; usually meetings and reports also do not require too much details.

In the knowledge economy, information is king, and this is precisely what keeps the employees valuable. Most companies have a suspicion that the 'well performing employees' may know much more than the other peers or the senior management, and therefore they always make efforts to retain that person, or use tactics like 'hear feedbacks for improvements' from such a person, before this person grows sick of the company and move out to a rival company. High value information may be hot leads that no one knows about, secret exclusive corporate news, competitors' costs, pricings and activities, brilliant strategies that could only be thought up by geniuses, and so on.

Most office workers these days are equipped with a personal computer, be it a desktop and/or a laptop, and for certain job functions (e.g. sales) also a mobile device. These are frequently used for data storage and communications, and the employee may have important or valuable information, or documents that are either stored in the files and folders; and even within messages or attachments on emails stored in the mailbox. These are the common targets for information theft and sabotages.

The most basic level of protection that any employee should mindfully practice is to set passwords for access to the devices and have security measures for logging in and out. It is good practice to always lock-screen whenever one is away from the computer, otherwise the computer is free for anybody's access when you are not around.

Information may not just be stolen, but it may even open up to scenarios whereby mischievous colleague can send nasty messages to the CEO via your email. If the IT policy allows, you should even transfer valuable information to a thumb drives or external storages (e.g. Google Drive) to keep it away from the devices that you are using (the employee should be careful about this, as some companies may prohibit such activities).

The next thing that one should do is to look at the physical desk and see if there are any documents that might have information that one does not want the rest to know. Sensitive documents should either be kept away (most common practice is lock and keys, but if your company allow you to bring these documents home, then jolly well do so), or if need be, shred them away.

If you are handling projects that are marked by progressive stages, sometimes you may run into the competitive colleague who may try to snoop around to suss out the progress you've made. When it comes to handling such a situation, it may pose a dilemma, because while you cannot lie about the progress- the truth always tend to reveal itself eventually and may open a pandora's box for contentions, you cannot also reveal too much information that might plant red flags.

One way to handle this is to 'Mask the Progress'. When asked such questions, you can choose to downplay the performance, and play up the struggles, while truthfully stating the level of progress. How does this work? Say you are working on a lead to close the sales, and you are at the 'Objections Stage' with a strong possibility of getting to the 'Closing Stage'. When asked about your progress, you can answer that you are facing tough objections from the key opinion leaders and is trying hard in handling them. In this answer, you truthfully mentioned the correct stage, played up the struggles with mentions about the difficulties, and downplayed the performance by not stating that you are moving closer to closing the sales.

Learn When to Shut Up

"Words like violence, breaks the silence." Many problems arise at work due to people not learning when to shut up. We have discussed earlier on about keeping opinions to oneself, reserving comments about co-workers, and the controlling of emotions. The key to making any of these successful is simply not to express them through verbal speeches.

Words are strong verbal signals that carry potency, regardless of whether the intended thought match up or not, because they are definitely taken at face value from the hearer or listener. People would automatically assume that the words are expressions of the thoughts from the speaker, and if the words are not well meaning, they have lasting effects.

Throughout the course of work, there are perhaps moments when you feel like saying something, as suggestions, criticisms, opinions. Make sure that these words make sense before they leave the mouth; because you can't unspeak those words that had been said, especially if they are damaging, erroneous, or provocative. The wise employee will often think through what needs to be said before the vocal cords vibrate. Think twice or even thrice on whether the words are sensible, meaningful, accurate or safe to say, to save you from regrets.

When you have nothing better to say, don't say anything at all. You may have the wildest punchline you formed in your head, the joke of the century which you feel like telling to the whole world, or feel the urge to comment on a subject matter which you are not too sure about, but want to feel important by saying something; still, cautiously you must, to assess the situation, context, environment, in case the words are inappropriate.

To reiterate, think twice, thrice, and save yourself from unnecessary problems that may arise from saying these words. By only saying few, but sensible comments, it may even work in favor with building up one's image, as a steadfast, sensible, mature and professional employee. On a more strategic front, silence is often used an invaluable tool in power play, by those who understand these rules of engagement.

Don't Shit Where You Eat

This is the last but not the least rule under "The Art of Concealment". For those who do not understand what the title means, it means 'do not get into romantic relationships with your co-workers'. This may not affect most employees, but we surely have heard of those few odd cases before; rumors and gossip about the two persons from the same office who behave more than colleagues.

While Cupid can strike anywhere, best to avoid that arrow if you can. If not, you've got to keep those affairs clandestine and hidden, or better still, leave the company altogether. It is usually perceived as highly scandalous when such relationships are discovered by the colleagues, between the two employees in the same office, regardless of whether the office has been used or not, because human beings thrive on such small minded gossip and rumors, and wild imaginations to spice up their otherwise boring existence.

Scandals can badly taint reputations and respectability, regardless of how proficient or capable the employee is, because he or she will be automatically relegated to object of shame in the eyes of the mean spirited mob, who may also serve to propagate such notions. Many of the worst downfall of great employees and/or leaders are precipitated by scandals.

Even when one has no romantic motives, one still needs to be extra careful when interacting with the opposite sex (or in some cases same sex). Late night in the office together with the person, frequent one on one lunch outings, or weekend outings have to be handled carefully, or simply best avoided; because all it takes is for someone to witness it, even when the two persons are not romantically involved or have done anything. That witness will most likely paint such sightings with scandalous allusions.

4. Projecting the Right Image

Style prevails over substance in our world because an average person has no time or patience to find out more. This is why human beings can be easily sold on images, like brands, celebrities, trends, fashion, Kardashians, so on and so forth, which may have little to no intrinsic value.

What is the right image then? It simply means an image that is acceptable, safe, and even welcoming. The right image can go a long way in any organization. Impressions are formed, and according to different sources, can range between under 1 second to a minute upon encounter. And when initial good impressions are formed, it also tends to stay on in the human's memory for quite a while.

People, as impressionable sheeples sold on images, judge everything first hand based on impressions. And by maintaining the right image consistently, things will definitely be easier, and even beneficial for the person at the workplace since it is a fact that often: acceptance and support by colleagues, recognitions and promotions by supervisors are based on what they think of the person, informed by how the person looks and behaves- impressions and images projected by the person's persona.

Cultivating the Right Image

You are perfectly fine to be who you are. But the people in the office may have different expectations. We are not recommending you to be a hypocrite, but rather to appear agreeable in the office. If you are a jovial person, then behave like a jovial professional. If you are a brooding person, likewise act like a brooding professional (while try to smile more often to brighten up your day and to increase likeability). As long as the professional image falls within a reasonable framework, it shouldn't be too difficult to follow, without compromising your personal values.

One who is highly adept in social skills knows this very well; about the projection of personas accordingly to different situations. The sort of persona projected to the office co-workers need not be exaggerated or contrived. The person should instinctively follow the expectations accordingly, so that one will not fall out of line. Obvious negative images to avoid need not be explained too much; it should never be offensive, or jeopardize the survival of oneself within the company.

We have talked about how a person who is compliant to the rules in the company, who has control over his or her own work, and who can work well in the job function is seen as an ideal employee. Many of the above are evinced and apparent over time; but the image at the outset, the very persona one should instantly cultivate is that of:

a) **a helpful person**- To appear helpful, even when one is really not. The colleagues rate others based on helpfulness. They will be nicer to you if you are proven to be helpful to them.

b) **an approachable person**- Who the colleagues can easily interact with, without difficulty.

c) **a modest person**- There should be no airs or threatening vibe.

d) **a considerate person**- Someone who will not bother the colleagues too much, when they are busy or when they have knocked off work.

e) **a seemingly competent person**- Note the word: seemingly- that means this person should look proficient enough for the job function so that the overall work can be properly done, but also not too competent to threaten the livelihood of the colleagues.

f) **a reasonable person**- One who is sensible, objective, rational and who speaks reason.

g) and very importantly, the **person should blend in rather well with the office crowd**, taking care not to stick out like a sore thumb. This should not be difficult as long as the person understands and maintains the need to behave professionally to enable work done better, and to be held in higher esteem (relative to the company).

Title
The Most Important Thing
In the Career

Ever wonder why many people never seem to get ahead in their career? No matter how much and how hard they worked, they can never seem to get promoted to a place of seniority, and thus still bear junior sounding titles. If they are perfectly fine with it, that's alright, but these people are sure as hell disgruntled. Perhaps they had followed the wrong advice, or focused working on things that did not improve their situations? Let's see what is going on.

If a person is on LinkedIn long enough, he or she may come across many platitudes dispensed by many so-called career gurus talking about how the most important thing in a person's career is not the job, nor the money, but the boss. They talk about the great wisdom in choosing the right boss for the job, and it is evidently something which can influence and affect the prospects of the employee.

Sure enough, in the last few decades or so, there were many pragmatic views that ultimately the money (from salary) is the most important determinant in the career, because that's the most tangible benefit which the employees can get. And this notion was somehow challenged in the last few years or so by the gurus, stating that in order to even get there, or ahead, the truly helpful and supportive bosses play very crucial roles.

This however needs to be updated. I had studied and examined many people with successful careers (and also with myself), and I found out that most people did not get a leg-up because of the supportive bosses. Rather, it was through the securing of 'Titles', titular or not. The pragmatic bunch fixated with salary may argue that a title is useless if the money does not match up. My response to this is that with titles, it can open up many avenues for opportunities in the job market, and may therefore lead to greater upsides, inclusive of the salary. And if the gurus argue what good can a person do with the title, if the boss is giving hell, I can simply reply that if the boss is giving hell, the title serves as a good tool to help the employee escape from this boss to greener pastures.

So what's with the title? A title bears the status or prestige of the employee, an affirmation for achievements and stages in the career. Human beings are superficial creatures; they tend to judge a person's career success and status based on titles. A senior person would rather talk to someone with the director title than say an assistant manager.

Inflated titles are handy if a person has not been bestowed one based on seniority. Yet, we have to be mindful on whether titles, especially inflated ones can be of any use in the industries. There is definitely no use for inflated titles in certain industries- e.g. in financial sectors, because every junior can be a vice president; but when it comes to other industries, it can be a tremendous opportunity booster because of the keywords therein. The missing link which connects the puzzle lies with- the recruiters, or the executive search firms.

Most of the executive search firms these days are using LinkedIn for candidate search. When they search on LinkedIn, they tend to focus on keyword searches. If they are looking for a Sales Manager in the Biomedical sector, they will do the Boolean 'and' operators on the terms: Sales, Manager and Biomedical. The benefit of securing a good title is to be able to be a result in that search. Senior title keywords for most of working adults are 'manager' and 'director', and are some of the most frequently searched terms by the executive search firms, because they are not entirely stupid people; they will want to work on more senior positions to get more commissions for the same amount of time used. Yet they can be stupid for the fact that they like to search laterally (they will find a manager candidate for a manager role in some other place).

If title is so important, then how can the feeble employee get there without recognition by bosses or promotions? This requires some strategy, which has worked well for me many times in the past.

Assuming Tom is just a junior sales executive, and having worked in a company for a year, he can consider talking to the boss to secure an external title for 'sales manager'. This of course has to be approached with certain caution, but it is a lesser known but legitimate corporate practice to enable the employee to secure an external title on the name card, while retaining the original title internally. Such practices are especially relevant in commercial settings, because the employee can claim that the external title will improve credibility and trust with the customers, especially if Tom is tasked with opening new markets. Dependent on the policies of the company, I have observed that most corporations are perfectly fine with this practice.

Yet this has to be approached with caution: if an employee is early in the job it is not advisable. Do check to see if the boss holds a more senior title than the title you are requesting for. If your boss is a manager, it is foolish to demand a manager title. Also, at any point if the bosses are not receptive to the idea of an external title, it has to be dropped.

Tom may still be a junior sales executive within his company, but his name card reflects the titular 'sales manager' even though he doesn't run a team under him, nor has the power or experience befitting of such a title.

But with this title, he opened up new career avenue for himself by calling himself a sales manager on LinkedIn, and rightfully so because it was an external title. Because of that, some recruitment company found him on LinkedIn, got him a job as a sales manager in the other company, and now he is a proper sales manager there, running a team of sales people. One should be like Tom, to think in the longer term, and not feel embarrassed securing an inflated title, because it can serve you well in the long run for your career.

Look Like You Care

So you may don't really care- about the company, colleagues and job. But it is imperative that you don't look like it, otherwise you are giving ammunition to your detractors. We understand what kind of bullshit most companies stand for: you are just a waged employee for a job function to facilitate their profiteering; but we also know very well that they would expect all employees to appear (real or not) to be into them.

It was previously discussed in 'What the Company Really Cares About" on the perceived values of the employees. Sometimes such assessment takes time, but superficially the wise employee should appear like that they uphold these values: Positive Numbers, Safety, Good Image, Smooth Operations; to create the image of loyalty, subservience, and emphasis on company/colleagues interests.

The wise employee can project this false image by acting proactive, showing interest in company's pointless missions and activities, faking upset when some bad news hit the company, and even getting gifts for the 'lovely' co-workers after a vacation. The costs are minimal, and there are usually huge upside behind this kind of behavior because it may even prove to be useful one day when the company starts evaluating on staff performances. Likewise, if one act like they don't care, the detractors can point out this fact when the going gets tough for the staff.

Be Punctual

Imagine this person turning up late to a meeting where the other participants were already seated there early, amused and annoyed by him or her making a late grand entrance.

There is nothing more annoying than a person who is late. In the professional setting, this is very frowned upon especially when it comes to meetings, and in many cases, work time. It is slightly rude to turn up too early, but it is considered very rude if the person is late without earlier notification or justifications.

It is definitely to the employee's advantage to cultivate the habit of timeliness. When a person is not punctual, he or she is viewed with displeasure. If the person has a habit of being late, he or she is held with utter disdain. The employee is always expected to be punctual, and a person who is recognized to be timely consistently, can be seen as a responsible, conscientious and organized person. These are definitely positive images that will ensure the survival and even the progress of this employee.

Keeping Proximity
And Never Be a Silo

When dealing with people, there is a constant need to estimate and assess proximity. Depending on the situation, it is appropriate to bring oneself closer, or further away from people. Ideally distances should be in the median, where one does not get unnecessarily close or far apart from a person, so that the employee can maintain his or her autonomy at arm's length, yet be approachable at the same time.

The dynamics of the office co-workers should be interdependent, because a function usually needs to be supported or give support to other functions, as well as the need for open communications and collaborations between co-workers to achieve certain goals. This means that certain closeness to the proximity of other co-workers are needed, as a team or interdepartmental effort. Yet at the same time, there is also a frequent need to observe boundaries, as each and every individual employees should rightfully have his or her own space without intrusion.

Problems arise when an employee does not has the right positioning in terms of proximity. When an employee is too far off and detached from other colleagues, he or she is giving off a signal of distance and unwillingness to cooperate or communicate. This may leave the employee in a vulnerable position, open to criticism, ostracization, and may lead to many misunderstandings which arise from imagined misgivings from the distant colleagues. However, when an employee gets too close or intimate with another colleague, he or she may be seen as intrusive, meddlesome, and this can sometimes lead to risky signals like giving the image of a nosy parker, a nuisance or worse, a creep.

As a general image, the employee should try to maintain a professional front: open and friendly to people, moderately helpful to colleagues (look at the topic of 'Restrict Helpfulness' to find out more), but distant enough to remain autonomous when it comes to own work functions, knowing and observing boundaries with the co-workers (like not calling them up during after work hours or weekends), and maintaining a healthy respect of the distance between oneself and the rest of the colleagues, with a slightly detached attitude. Sometimes with a little bit of detachment, it adds to the allure of a person as it gets people fascinated.

On the other hand, an employee should never ever get into a silo situation An isolated employee is a most vulnerable one; it does not give that sense of allure or mystery like a slightly detached person, but rather the image of a lonely loser. An isolated, and non-communicative, unfriendly and unhelpful antisocial can get the colleagues annoyed, repulsed, and worse still, the lone wolf may find it hard to get help if needed, or to redeem oneself even if he or she wanted to be sociable later, because the colleagues would have already formed a bad impression.

Act Like a Team-Player

It was mentioned in the previous topic about defining and keeping proximity with the co-workers. Getting too close or too far away from colleagues may bring about undesirable outcomes, but that is entirely up to the individual. Yet, the company expects the employees to close the gap and close ranks with one another, so that they can effectively function as a team. And they will not like it if it is not the case.

There must be a reason why some of the companies (especially the bigger ones) are willing to spend huge amounts of money, resources and time, on teambuilding and other equally costly, redundant and useless pursuits to bring everyone in the organization closer to one another.

If you can recall, in 'What the Companies Really Care About' under "The Red Pill", I talked about how companies do care about 'Smooth Operations'- which means that business processes can be performed smoothly without hiccups. If the employees and/or departments are disconnected and uncooperative, it will definitely lead to downtime and hiccups, which will affect the processes. In order to make the flow of processes more seamless, much teamwork needs to be in place.

In order not to get regarded as uncooperative, anti-social or even disruptive, the wise employee should consciously keep up the image of a team-player. One can begin by being receptive and open to answering requests (yet this must not go overboard- refer to "Restrict Helpfulness') and have some friendly interactions with the co-workers.

During meetings or discussions, always make it a point to address the team for all efforts, using "we" instead of "I". Sometimes, one may also need to oblige to participate in team activities and socialize in company outings.

For the more ambitious, one can start looking out to the 'Five Departments', discussed in "Knowing the Other Departments" to start networking with them on improving existing interdependent functions. The top dogs in the higher management tend to like efforts like this.

Do Not Assume Villain Persona

This is a folly made by many who are obsessed by their quest to become powerful and respected in their workplace. You can't really blame them; they probably watched too much TV. In modern popular culture we are often bombarded with somewhat misguided association between cruel, conniving and nasty behavior with efficiency, resiliency and success. The problem is that the gullible took this association literally and wore this bluff in order to appear tougher.

Even if a person is a genuine nasty character, it is still rather foolish to show it. People often act like that to intimidate people, to command respect, either looking intentionally aggressive, hard to deal with, and even performing conspicuous acts of hostility because somehow they think that they can inspire fear to make co-workers or subordinates (or even bosses) to respect them or carry out their work. But it is actually a very unwise thing to do, especially if the person is not in the position of sufficient power or new to a company.

Chances are you already know what the villain persona looks like if you've enough watched Disney cartoons or seen any Hollywood productions in your life; the images and demeanor of those villains always carry an exaggerated vileness, wicked smirks, narrowing eyes, low coarse Gollum-like whispers, or rude behavior at people (vulgarities, shouts), and rubbing hands together (yes). While those are theatrical expressions of wickedness, people who assumed these appearances thought they would be on the right track to becoming the quintessentially psychopathic CEO.

One minor thing that I also observe power imitators do: not using salutations when addressing a person in emails (i.e. email that opens with the first name of the person.) This is typically inculcated in not-so-successful middle management to sound authoritative, curt and to the point, disregarding needs of formality. This practice is just plain right stupid, especially if the email is addressed to a superior. Usually people can instantly feel annoyed at the lack of respect, and the insecure contrivance projected from such email, and will tend to harbor resentful thoughts towards such a person.

Most of the time, over-the-top act of aggressive/authoritarian tactics always certainly backfire on the people who practiced it, usually leading to growing political rivalry, premature dismissal and even the end of their career (remember, news can spread to other organizations).

I had mentioned before that true power cannot be easily discerned, otherwise it is not true power. What truly instils fear and respect is the unknown, the unpredictability of the power which a person can yield. Sometimes we see those tough acting career women putting on their red "power" suit to appear on top of their game; in reality it has no real power as they are showing their intent and insecurities, and they themselves may likely turn into targets of ridicule.

Watch Out for
Passive Aggressive Gestures

In recent years, I noted this rather stupid trend of people performing fist palming (not palm fisting..) openly, in the presence of who would be considered as important to them, oblivious to the negative connotations it carries. If you've not heard of fist palming before, it is a universally obscene gesture where a person swings a fist from one hand into the palm of the other hand, like a proverbial "fuck you".

Many thought that this is cool to do when they are standing around in the company of others. I have seen so many instances when the subordinates were swinging away in the presence of their bosses! Even if this is not intended, it is a hostile, passive aggressive cue which suggests insecurity and irritation. Most of the time, the recipient would interpret this negatively, and categorize you into his/her blacklist.

There are many other passive aggressive cues, and fist palming is only one of them. One of the other infamous one is "The Catapult", which is essentially putting both palms behind the back of the head, usually to imply superiority, coolness and confidence while it really carries a message of defiance, and the superior usually senses it. Other negative cues to watch out for are the hands-on-hips, arms folding, yawns, stares, rolling eyes, shoulder shrugs.

Consider Your Body

Unless you are a model, chances are you probably have average body and looks. The average body and looks comes in all shapes and sizes and there are certainly no stringent expectations in maintaining very high standards in one's outlook in the normal office setting. There are however certain stereotypes which are associated with ones' outlook in the professional sense, especially when it comes to the body sizes. While a person is not able to change much of the looks aside from applying cosmetics (unless one takes drastic measures like plastic surgery); a person's body shape and size can still be changed, never mind if one is genetically predisposed to be an ectomorph or endomorph, and the employee may see the need to consider such changes if the stereotypes are affecting their career.

The professional image is actually not demanding for the average folks: the employee does not has to look like a muscular hunk or a curvy babe in order to make the cut. He or she can look like any average Joe or Jane and perfectly get away with it. By this, the norm is a relatively slim body, with allowance for paunch and flabbiness to set in as the person gets on with age. But the unfortunate employee, especially male employees frequently bear the brunt of severe stereotypes. Surprisingly, people tend to view women in a more forgiving light, but men who deviates from the standard body size are highly stereotyped even when most people do not consciously realize this.

Societal expectations of a younger male person are about thier vitality and enthusiasm. When a younger male employee presents himself as obese and sluggish, he could be unfortunately typecast, consciously or subconsciously by his fellow colleagues . You see, the problem does not lie with the fact that people do get plus sized; indeed many plump and spritely males do get extremely popular in the office. But younger men who look obese and sluggish exude the opposite of this vitality and enthusiasm; he may be immediately viewed upon as lazy, unmotivated, low energy, incompetent, unhealthy and even unlucky.

On the other hand, and on the extreme opposite of the spectrum, men who look like they are flaunting their muscular biceps and six packs are also stereotyped. Muscular men bears a different type of stigma; for some reason, especially in modern societal context, they are either associated with himbos or more frequently, as homosexuals. This is extremely unfair for the health conscious men, but unfortunately, such stereotypes persist, especially in the office, and in turn the employee may become a subject of gossip and ridicule.

It is definitely unjust and discriminatory for such stereotypes to persist, but persist they will, for people are still rather small minded and judgemental. The above examples are only some of such stereotypes; people can be generally unkind towards most deviation from norm. In this topic, I must clarify that it is rather cautionary, than a mandatory advice.

Dressing Appropriately

A person is judged very often based on his or her appearance, starting from the clothes and accessories which they are wearing. Women co-workers tend to pay more attention to such details on the targeted person (starting from shoes, then handbags, dress and accessories to try to reconcile the objects with the person's face and body), whereas men are less particular about this, unless threatened (e.g. sharp looking young upstart).

The rule of dressing appropriately is to always dress like the rest of the people in the office; the key is to fit in, to blend in to the herd, and not to draw unnecessary attention to yourself. Dress up or dress down according to the requirement and convention of the office.

If you belong in a standard office, standard work outfits are recommended, as long as they are appropriate, clean, decent; and not gaudy, eccentric, revealing. Sloppy, dirty dressing is definitely out (unless you are working in a labour intensive job; but that's usually not in the office), but surprisingly it is actually less offensive than over-the-top expensive dressing.

Unless the nature of the job demands one to dress sharply (lawyers, investment bankers for example), it may not always be appropriate in a regular deskbound work environment. People who dresses too sharply or too expensive are often perceived by other co-workers as show-offs or someone who lack substance, especially if that person is someone from a lower level in the company.

Dressing too sharply is also frowned upon in more technology driven units or businesses (IT, support, applications), and even within commercial departments of a technical company, whereby there is a commonplace prejudice that salespeople who dress well are airheads with more style than substance.

On the other spectrum, if the worker is in a more business or customer facing setting which cares about professional image (consultants, investment bankers, lawyers), then it is really worth investing more time and money on the wardrobe. Sloppy dressings are especially frowned upon in this circle, because their employers expect them to carry and represent the best image of the company, especially when it comes to meeting with customers.

Next comes the "Casual Friday" concept. Not every company practices that, but if your company does; do not abuse this concept. It usually means dressing down into "Smart Casuals", and not something sloppy like home clothes or sleep wears. By "Smart Casuals" it usually means jeans or polo-tees or blouses, but no T-shirts and short-pants. Also, if you are meeting customers on Friday, it is best to revert back to normal office wears to maintain that professional touch and courtesy.

The Handshakes

Most self-help books claim strong firm handshakes indicate confidence. However, what they failed to mention is that strong, crushing handshakes will certainly backfire and make one seem brutal, insecure and eager to prove a point, and therefore considered a hostile move. Soft/gentle handshakes may come across as insincere or weak, but surprisingly actually the most powerful people has the limpest handshakes. By not going overboard on either approaches above, it is always best to maintain a moderate strength handshake with a certain amount of firmness.

One point to take note of in any handshake is on whether it is too cold, clammy or wet. When a handshake is performed under such conditions, the other party almost immediately gets hygiene or even health concerns. Therefore, it is important to keep the palms dry and warm. If you are the type with sweaty palms, or the anxious types with cold hands and feet, it is best to have a handkerchief in the pockets. Before performing a handshake, put the hand into the pocket and squeeze on the handkerchief; it will raise the temperature of the hand and also dry the sweaty palms.

The Secret Art of Smiling

Depending on what effects a person want to achieve, there should not be one formula to follow when it comes to smiling. The many self-help books out there talk about the powerful positive image of the Duchenne Smile, also termed the "Genuine Smile" because it involves the raising of corners of mouth, and cheeks to create a "smile with smiling eyes". This is usually a sign of a smile with genuinely positive emotions and it is certainly viewed positively by the recipient, but yet it is not something that should be frequently performed in the work environment.

The Duchenne Smile should be reserved only for merry occasions, as a response to good news or jokes, or when meeting a new colleague or boss for the first time. If used too often, especially when you are pulling bluffs, the mind will tend to forget to coordinate the cheek muscles to create the effect of the "smiling eyes", and reduce your smile into a "Fake Smile", meaning to say a face with a smile but unsmiling eyes, with an insincere vibe.

The "Fake Smile" is quite commonly practiced in offices throughout the world as an act of fake approval and diplomacy, and it is easy to tell the difference from a genuine smile. A person (especially man) with fair, delicate facial features should take note, that the "Fake Smile" on such a face will create a heightened level of distrust (reinforcing image as a backstabber) in the eyes of the other party. Also, other obviously negative smiles like lop-sided smirks and grimaces (sick desperation they say) should be avoided by all when possible.

There is a smile that many self-help books consider negative, but is actually the most effective smile when shown to a superior. And that is the close-lipped smile with positive body languages (earnest look in the eyes, and head nods in agreement). Why is this so? The close-lipped smile, which involves the slight curling up of lower lip under the upper lip is a sign of "smiling through pain". However, coupled with positive body language, it creates the subliminal image/illusion of genuine compliance and to the superior.

The general rule is that if there is no need to smile, don't smile. It is ok to smile when meeting your colleagues at the corridor, hearing good news, or lightening up in conversations. However, if a person smiles too often, he or she is regarded as creepy, fake or even slightly mental.

The Approving Nod
One of the Best
Body Language To Use

If there is one definitive body language to use, it is the "Approving Nod". There are of course many positive gestures available, but this one has its special place as not many people are aware of how powerful it can be.

When this is performed while the other party (especially bosses) are talking, this is the most obvious "positive" gesture that can be seen at the eye level, and will almost subliminally send a signal of approval and agreement to the other party, making them feel appreciated.

The head should preferably nod at small angle to the neck; large, exaggerated swing makes the person unctuous, insincere, even mildly passive aggressive. The nods can be greatly enhanced by the index finger and thumb clipping the chin, giving the impression/illusion that you are really impressed, therefore stoking the ego of the other party, and making them like you better.

Making a Point
With Finger & Thumb

"Finger pointing" is an idiom for blaming (whether literally or not) and we are not discussing this conceptually here. Rather, we are going to be talking about the usage of fingers to make a point.

The literal finger pointing (extending out the index finger from the rest of the clenched fist in the direction of somebody) is outright accusatory/censuring and a very dangerous gesture to be made especially when the finger pointer is making a point with some people of higher authority.

Sometimes during meetings or presentations, the speaker gets carried away and unknowingly wave the index finger when stressing a point. In order to mitigate the harmful effects of such a hand gesture, the astute person can seal the tip of the index finger with the tip of the thumb, into a shape of a pincer. With this gesture, the offensive element is removed, and it will actually create an effect of thoughtfulness, accuracy and intellect to the audience when the speaker make a point.

Watch Your Decibel, Tone, Speech Rate and Accent

Theodore Roosevelt (26th President of the United States) once said, "speak softly and carry a big stick; you will go far" as a statement of his approach on foreign policy. This phrase purportedly originated from Africa and had been used to describe how successful hunters thrived in the dangerous jungles filled with wild beasts. In a way, the office is not much different from the jungles, and colleagues are also not different from the beasts, because your survival can greatly depend on the sound you make and what effects it has on the animals.

By watching your decibel, tone, speech rate and accent, it will save you from creating negative impression or draw unnecessary attention whenever you speak. It may not be just a matter of what you talk about, but how you speak them. A seemingly harmless comment can be interpreted with great repulsion if spoken in a certain manner. That's why many great leaders of the world are mindful of this and practiced this well.

Decibel- The sound volume of your talking

   a) Loud: When a person talks loudly in the office, he/she is generally regarded as somewhat oafish or arrogant by other colleagues with more quiet dispositions. Unless one strategically favors to acquaint oneself to similarly loud and boisterous company (high-energy people sometimes like such camaraderie; if your boss talks loudly, it is safe to talk loudly, you may even be inducted into the inner circle), it is always safer to restrain from making such rackets.

b) Soft: On the other hand, it is also not really appropriate to speak too softly. It tends to make people think that the speaker is weak or secretive, and chances are whatever has been said needs to be repeated again due to inaudibility.

Of the two, being loud is likely to offend more than being soft. Moderate to slightly lower volume works best for most employees. There is a technique of power from top management which makes use of switching volumes to create authority. Speech is usually carried out at mid volume, but it will get softened (and slowed down) to make serious points, or gradually loudened to show annoyance. This is however, exclusive for senior management.

Tone- How your speech sounds like

It is generally divided into two parts, namely Pitch and Attitude.

1. Pitch-
   a) High Pitch: Sounding shrill and cheery. Next time when you have a chance to observe the irritating sycophants

in your company, note how they tend to raise the pitches in their voice when they are talking to important leaders in the company. This is a natural response from most human beings when they are talking to someone they perceive as more superior, and therefore they subconsciously and subserviently pander to their imaginary masters, because a higher pitch usually connotes the notion of friendliness and earnest. This is safe and even encouraged to practice when one is in a position of servitude or the lower ranks in the company; this tend to boost the ego of the superiors on the other side, while watching pathetic slobbering slaves trying hard to please the demigods, and for that, the lowly slaves may sometimes be lifted up in ranks. However, when the employee finally rose up to the ranks of middle manager and beyond, the high pitch thing has to be done away, and the more appropriate pitch of choice is a lower one.

b) Low Pitch: Sounding baritone and solemn. Lower pitch creates more gravitas, and therefore boosts the employee's street cred. However, if you are a staff of rather low rank, it creates the impression of you as a robotic servant, especially if you also speak slowly.

2. Attitude- How your voice suggests what you are thinking or feeling. As a general rule, strive to sound positive, reasonable, objective, enthusiastic (if presented a challenge, otherwise remain somewhat relaxed) and friendly in a measured manner (the Mahatma Gandhi kind of friendly, not the Barney the Dinosaur kind of friendly). Negative attitude is easily picked

up by most people and they will surely create instant aversion. These are negative Tone Attitudes that are ranked from the worst in descending order.

a) Fear Tone- The worst of them all. This means that the tone of the talking has a certain dread and worry that makes the person seem weak and unable to control the situation. Anxiety and fear are like trails of blood that can be sniffed out by would be predators and other manifestations of the detractors, to pinpoint convenient weak spot to zero in and attack. Some examples of the "Fear Tone" is to stammer out of anxiety, to literally "choke on your words" or to incessantly sound helpless, defeated or worried.

b) Hostile Tone- Ranges from sounding angry, to sounding sarcastic or curt. This is an off-putting tone that can only offend. Never do this to one's superior as it can come across as impudent and challenging the authority.

c) Defensive Tone- This occurs very frequently and most people aren't even aware they are actually doing it. When a person is known to frequently answer questions with, 'but', 'actually', or interrupt conversations with 'no....', this person can be deemed as defensive, and also a little bit of an opinionated fool.

d) Impatient Tone- This may not be picked up as readily as the aforementioned, but yet many people are guilty of it. Common examples are answering someone with "ya, ya, ya", or ending a phone conversation with "bye, bye, bye". As innocuous as they may sound, they are certainly not 'three times the charm'. It's ok to perform the bluff of sounding impatient once in a while to the office when you are in the midst of major projects because you "care so much", although in reality you may not give a shit. This impatience bluff is best laden with a tinge of "anger" than "anxiety", as the latter is a favorite of predators.

e) Asinine Tone- It simply means sounding stupid but it can also be extended into sounding sluggish, inane, childish, uninspired and inappropriate. Tendency to say "huh?" will seal the fate of the unfortunate office dunce. If you are unable to NOT sound stupid, try not to say anything at all.

Speech Rate- How fast does one speak, and how it is paced

It is vital for conveying the speech properly.

a) Talking Fast: While fast talking usually is a sign of intelligence, talking too fast can be detrimental to the image of the person. First thing that will happen, some messages will surely be lost at the receiving end. Secondly, it can make the speaker look like overly confident novice and a bit of the salesman wheeler dealer type who are too keen to show off their language dexterity without actual substance. Either way, it works against the speaker so it should be avoided at all cost.

b) Talking Slow: Talking slower is better than too fast, but not slow enough until the conversation drags on painfully. When a person speaks too slowly, the audience will be bored to tears, and also somehow reinforce the image of one that is low energy and not too intelligent. It is recommended that normal employees do normal speed talking, but when one gets into a higher level of power and beyond, it helps to speak slightly slower than normal. Look at the leaders in your organization, or successful political leaders on TV; they speak like that, with well timed pauses to augment their thoughtfulness.

Accent- How one pronounces a language

People sometimes pull phony accent to connect with other people from different cultures, status or background. But, it is wise to never assume a phony accent because your cover will surely be blown. When non-native speakers pull phony accent, most native recipients are not impressed and will think that they try too hard, or even as offensive (mocking at certain accent). Just look at how Hillary Clinton's accents changed throughout the years.

On the other hand, efforts to speak non-mother tongue languages properly and grammatically correct, with a genuine local accent is more welcoming and often deemed as sincere.

Grow a Thick Skin
(Or Faking It)

If you easily get slighted or blushed when people say offensive, embarrassing or upsetting things to you, maybe it is time to learn tactics or even make changes to deal with it.

There is this thing about people; if they are highly sensitive, chances are they also tend to show it. When the people read the change of mood through your facial expressions, your tone, your attitude; they can almost instantaneously pick it up and recognize the trigger and the weak spot of the person.

The more mean spirited individuals will definitely revisit this trigger to push again on the same buttons to attack and wear the person down. And they certainly will be able to get away with it, because a highly sensitive person tend to also not react well during the disturbed state of mind, and may react inappropriately, thus falling for the traps laid by the antagonist.

Most of the time though, the criticism, or the comments may not be personally directed at the sensitive person, but the latter may take them too seriously or regarded with imagined threats. But even if someone is deliberately poking at the weak spot of the individual, the person should still learn to grow a thick skin and deal with it. Having a thick skin doesn't mean that one doesn't react to the insulter or to put up with suffering injustice; these may actually be seen as signs of cowardice or resigning/submitting to the antagonist. Rather, a thick skin is to look like the insults or actions have 'no effects', or even 'positive effects' to the individual. By positive effects, it means that the individual can even seem amused by the remarks.

There are several advantages with having a thick skin:

1.) It will actually surprise the offensive party, especially if they deliberately are out to hurt. When they realize that the person is seemingly unaffected or even responded well to the remark or action, they will start to realize that their offensive have failed and that this person is certainly more than who he or she seem to be.

2.) The offensive party will have a mix of fear and respect to this individual. It takes great amount of reticence, self control and even cunning to withstand insults and emerging unfazed. These qualities also make the offensive party realize that they are not dealing with a novice or pushover, but a potentially powerful person.

3.) It will save you from clouding your mind and making mistakes. When a person get too angry or upset by the remarks or actions, sometimes he or she may react in inappropriate ways which may even undermine his or her professionalism.

Growing a thick skin may sound easier said than done, especially when you are a highly emotional, sensitive and direct person. However, it is still possible to 'Fake it'. Here are some recommendations which could help you to fake a thick skin. First, let's begin with a cynical mindset: to see people as opportunistic idiots who will try every means and ways to undermine your profession (although to be fair, there could be constructive criticisms that come from a good place). Next, have a comedic image of the office. There are idiots in the midst and they will try desperate tricks on you. You are beyond them, and they will end up looking like clowns when they fail.

After you are conditioned with these thoughts, the next time you encounter an antagonist trying to say mean things to you, you could do the following:

1) Rest your top eyelid and make it fall, to make your eyes look like half awake. Do not narrow your eyes, as it may look hostile, but simply just relax it, like how you look when you have a nice cold beer. This action will subconsciously inform the brain to shut out signals, and make a person more relaxed. The other party will feel like you seem either tired or unimpressed by his or her remarks or actions.

2) With the relaxed state of mind, conjure the comedic image you had made on the office folks. Then imagine a big red clown nose on the face of the antagonist.

3) If you do not want to unsettle the other party, at this stage you can continue the conversation. Otherwise you can taunt the antagonist with a soft smile on your relaxed face because of the amusing way he or she looked like a clown, and if necessary, walk away smiling (or laughing).

Restrict Helpfulness
(But Always Appear Helpful)

The colleague who offered to clear trash in the first week into the job, may likely continue to do so for the rest of the office life, because most of the co-workers will gladly hand over their trash to this person; the latter usually have to suck it up and oblige because he or she was a newbie initially and this habit had been cast in stone for posterity. Looking at the heuristics of the organization, whereby it is wired around proximity and leverage; if someone can fulfil function X, that person will automatically be assumed as an X drone, no thanks attached.

At the outset, it is always best practice to be mindful about how your first week in the job can have an effect for the rest of your office life. Unless the employee is instructed to perform obligatory duties, there is no need to play nice and 'go beyond'. Also, one should be conscious about other habits and behavior during the initial period, so as not to encourage unnecessary dependency. For example, Mary who behaved empathetic may attract the company of miserable people who will gladly load their misery onto her. John who is so keen to help colleagues who are struggling with spreadsheet problems automatically turned into the go-to person for all Excel problems in the office, which is beyond his normal duty. If precedent caution was made earlier on, Mary and John would not have to deal with these problems; unless they sincerely wanted to.

Yet if you read an earlier rule within this chapter, 'Cultivating the Right Image', I mentioned that the employee should always 'appear' helpful. The unhelpful type is universally hated in all offices, and surely not a good behavior to maintain for long term survival.

One way to resolve the dilemma above is to only offer help when one is capable and when the situation is necessary, and one should learn to stop when the deed is done. If someone comes along to request for similar help again, it is reasonable to pretend to look busy, and appearing like your plate is full, thereby rejecting politely and subtly if you can, citing work problems or commitments to handle, whether real or not, and chances are that person would not come back to bother. Also help should be dispensed selectively to the people who are capable of ensuring your success (and one should be calculative about potential benefits from such helpful gestures thereafter); universal altruism may earn you certain fame and admiration but usually more for your moral standing than your competency.

In "The Daily Grind" under the topic 'Ask For Help When Needed', I will talk about how the two opposite rules in 'Cultivating the Right Image' and here, are in fact essentially similar, and how one will need to mindfully tread these rules carefully to achieve the best results. Because help tend to be reciprocal in human term; one will tend to get help only when he or she has helped.

Looking Busy vs
Appearing Effortless

When the going gets tough, it may show on the employee. Many self-help books teach the employee to try to appear unfazed when faced with too much works or too hard works, so as to give people the impression that the person is too good, or the work is a piece of cake to that person. However, this is not always a good strategy to utilize. Why is this so? We shall look into it in greater details.

Understandably, any person who shows the stress face, or complain about his or her work is easily seen as incapable in the eyes of the bosses and the colleagues. But the person who appears busy will not actually be affected by such views, and may actually stand to gain more than lose.

The very important part to avoid when the going gets tough, is to not make it evident that you are actually crumbling under pressure from the work. That means no visible sign of losing control/getting into a mess, and not getting affected mentally and emotionally.

When one seems busy because of work, there are actually several subliminal cues which are sent out in the process:

a) that the person is diligent (thereby satisfying the boss, the management and placating the colleagues),

b) that the person's plate is full (so the boss will not try to assign more tasks, and the colleagues will not try to bother the person for help),

c) can be used to redeem oneself should these efforts fail later. Sometimes even when the employee is not busy, it still works greatly to his or her advantage to pretend to be busy, precisely to benefit from above advantages.

On the other hand, appearing effortless too often may make the employee earn the reputation as a whiz kid, but may not necessarily make the immediate boss, counterpart or competitive colleagues comfortable, due to varying reasons from insecurity to envy and paranoia (remember the rule in "Art of Concealment"- Hide Your Shine?). If one intends to impress people by making work look effortless, the right kind of audience should be chosen selectively, like the bosses of the boss, the top dogs in the company.

Display Minor Weaknesses

I have explained before in "Hide Your Shine" about how disadvantageous it is for people who appear too perfect. Many self-help books recommends the average employee to aspire towards such an appearance, but they do not caution on the ill consequences that this can cause. A person who appears too perfect is a magnet for envy, competition and insecurity. In this topic here, while we discuss about the projection of right image, we should also incorporate a certain level of dampener on perfection.

One key dampener to utilize, especially for the strongly competent employee, is to learn how to have display of minor weaknesses. In an earlier topic 'Hide Your Weaknesses', I have explained the need to conceal away apparent weaknesses. But what I am proposing here is not a contradicting statement, but rather a measured approach towards projection of image by precisely using weaknesses. By all means, real apparent weaknesses should still be hidden away when possible. What I am suggesting here is the creation of 'minor weaknesses' to lower the guard of the co-workers.

Minor weaknesses, as the name imply, are lesser faults which do not make the person look weak and incompetent. It should be a non-threatening shortcoming which is harmless, but obvious enough to appease the scrutinizing colleagues. Some examples of minor weaknesses are obsession over safe and acceptable interests and harmless idiosyncrasies. At a subconscious level, the co-workers will think that this person is as equally fallible and flawed as the rest of the colleagues, and therefore do not then perceive the person as a threat.

To illustrate the point, let's say Gerald, an accountant, is seated in close proximity to the other colleagues within the finance team. He is a brilliant accountant, very meticulous and diligent but he frequently chews on the tip of the pen when thinking hard. Most co-workers noticed that, but they dismissed it as just one of the idiosyncrasies of Gerald, without finding him a threat, because he seemed like a regular guy (because of his habits). Gerald on the other hand, harbors ambitious plan to become the head of department.

Raise Visibility Carefully

I have talked enough about "Hide the Shine"- to not attract unnecessary attention. However, the reverse of this rule can be applied to exclusive situations, to make you stand out from the crowd and to attract the attention of those who may be able to help you advance in your career. This strategy relies on projecting your visibility to the right crowd. Who are the wrong crowd in this approach? They are: your fellow colleagues, and your boss. And the right crowd are: the Top Dogs who are more senior than you; bosses of your boss, and other departments.

Most other self-help books on career development always emphasize on raising one's visibility, with no concern on the negative consequences which can arise if these efforts backfire. The wise employee should know that any of these efforts should be discerning and concentrated on worthwhile targets, otherwise it is a waste of time, resources and even a potential career ending mistake. In front of the immediate boss and fellow colleagues, one should observe those points I made in 'Cultivating the Right Image':

a) be approachable, b) be modest, c) be seemingly competent, d) be reasonable and e) blend into the office like everyone else.

Towards the boss specifically, one should also observe these points I made in 'Knowing the Boss':

a) bring no trouble or problem, b) bring not too much bad news, c) complete tasks on time, d) make the boss look good, e) do not complain or seek too much help, e) do not steal thunder, f) respect the authority, g) stay away from boss's superior or enemies, h) to be on the same side during political games.

However, when it comes to the Top Dogs, bosses of bosses and other departments; it is necessary to have additional points to showcase:

a) deliver the current function well, and able to improve on it,

b) ability to seamlessly make cross departmental functions flow well,

c) has a business growth mindset as well as the strategies, for improving the company,

d) ability to speak their languages, and most importantly,

e) demonstrably better than the immediate boss in performance, management and even leadership.

In order to bring across all these points to these targets, one need to plan out how to raise the visibility, in a way which will not prematurely backfire upon oneself when the immediate boss or colleagues find out. It may seem like an impossible task for one to be able to raise visibility to these targets because one definitely has to observe the chain of command, which I have explained in 'Knowing the Hierarchy', as well as the fact that these people may be too far distally removed from where one is (especially if you are a junior staff), and that the boss and the other colleagues are constantly in close proximity. Yet there are strategies that will enable one to do so.

I will elaborate more later on in the book on specific strategies to do so. But for now, one plausible avenue to raise visibility is to 'impress the heads of other departments', especially if you are in a job function which has interdepartmental interactions. Let's leave out the bosses of the boss for now and focus on the other departments.

There is always a likelihood that the other departments have certain "conflict points" when it comes to dealing with the department you belong in. Do you have insights and solutions to bridge these problems? If you have, do not announce them, but simply implement them subtly in your interaction with the other departments and they will definitely take note.

Let me illustrate an example: Gary is working as a technical support specialist in the services and support department in an engineering firm. The service and support department has a boss named Gabriel, as well as many support staff who often made excuses and delayed on servicing faulty instruments in the accounts, when the account managers from the sales team made the requests. Gary, knowing how unpopular his department is when it comes to rendering support; acted more proactive in servicing the instruments, reaching out to the account managers from the sales team. For this, Spencer, the head of the sales team knows that Gary is the best person to work with from the services and support team (and better than Gabriel), and therefore recognizes and even raises attention of Gary to Michael, the senior manager, who is his immediate boss, as well as the immediate boss of Gabriel. There is a certain risk that Gabriel will discover such recommendation, but by then it will be too late. Gabriel will find it hard to give too much trouble to Gary, because he has the backing of both Spencer and Michael.

Protect Your Reputation

Despite all the upkeep of images, it only takes few minor stains to taint and tarnish your reputation, along with all the good images which you have built up.

When a person's reputation is tarnished, it can have long term lasting effects. News will surely spread, many times beyond the confines of the office, throughout the whole company, and even into the market and the industry.

A damaged reputation may hurt the employee's prospects for career development, job finding and applications. We always have to bear in mind that the industry can be a small place (every participants are somewhat linked in the whole professional circle); and people tend to enjoy gossip and rumor mongering to propagate any sort of misdeeds which might have occurred.

Therefore, always remember to protect your reputation, at all costs. There are several things which can hurt a person's reputation. The first of it is your general work performance. In order to earn a bad reputation due to poor work, the level of performance is usually astoundingly poor; because even the most mediocre workers tend not to attract such attention. The next thing is concerning your general work ethics and attitude. If one has compromised his or her work efforts by misdemeanor, bad attitude and/or dishonesty, this can have a tremendous effect in lowering the credibility of the worker, potentially raising red flags in the view of this person. The last but not the least is scandals. These scandals are often not related to work, but a stain on the personal lives of the employee. Perhaps it has got to do with the untimely romance in the office, or bad behavior that was caught by someone outside of the working hours; these are even more damaging to a person's reputation, because people tend to remember these details well.

In order to get away from potential infamy and notoriety, the employee should be constantly vigilant and mindful of the way he or she interacts with the members in the company, how he or she should behave outside of work, sidestepping potential landmines and entrapment, behaving in a professional and appropriate manner, take control of the emotions (especially if the person is emotional or reactionary), and pay attention to see if any rules and laws (written or unspoken) have been transgressed in the process.

5. The Daily Grind

Much of modern office work is repetitive and monotonous motion. 80% of the time will involve a personal computer (mostly writing and replying emails, Excel, Word and Powerpoint preparations) and the rest of it are meetings, discussions, and paper filing. These largely constitute the daily grind, but there may be some deviations here and there, depending on the nature of the work and industry. However, most desk bound employees tend to do the aforementioned on a frequent basis.

The daily grind can be boring and tiresome, or comfortably numb. Most people tend to get used to it after a while, unless disrupted by work emergencies and carpal tunnel syndrome. Because of the repetitive nature of work, human beings will eventually develop habits which revolve around their preferred work style, and which can come as a second nature.

These habits can become a permanent fixture in the person, unless he or she is consciously changing them. The habits can be good, bad or neutral, and they certainly affect the employee to a certain degree. As a general guide, good habits involve planning, caution and efficiency. Bad habits are more haphazard, risky and sloppy. The latter would certainly place the employee in a more disadvantageous position within an organization.

In order to minimize mistakes, reduce problems, and maximize work performance and even raise credibility, it is crucial to examine how one has been doing his or her work all along, and critically pinpoint potential bad habits and see if there are means to change them.

As I mentioned earlier, there are three key factors which are characterized as good habits, and which are also factors influencing work functions, namely planning, caution and efficiency. Planning as the name simply suggest, is to have proper planning for work done, especially when it comes to projects. Caution involves care and attention to mistakes, inaccuracies, and even at a human level (e.g. will the work bring inconvenience to some people). Efficiency looks at whether a task can be performed in the least resource consuming, and most expedient way with the best results.

Based on the above, we can see how the daily grind, can affect an employee's job in a profound way. It is a case of the means justify the ends; the constant grind will bring an employee to some kind of outcome at a certain point in their career. Rather than to mindlessly plod along, it is always prudent to be mindful of the effects it can bring.

Planning Ahead

People always talk about how luck is an important factor in ensuring success in their endeavor. We would like to think that way, but we should also consider the possibility that luck may not be as intangible as having the stars aligned. In my opinion, and through my experiences, I am always inclined to believe that there is a certain formula to luck; a summation of 50% planning and preparation, 10% timing, 30% hard work, and 10% force majeure (perhaps that's when the stars are aligned).

As you can see, the most important component for luck (and success) lies in planning and preparation at 50%. I separate that from hard work, specifically to highlight a precursor before the actual work, and if we must sum up the both, it can be up to 80% of hard work we are talking about here, since it definitely requires a certain amount of work to make plans and prepare. A person who behaves reactionary to work and situations tend to not succeed and may even end up looking stupid; when a person plans ahead, this quality can be evinced through the measured approach in dealing with the work and situations and they stand a higher chance of succeeding, which may then serve as a luck paradigm.

Planning and preparation should always be inculcated as a practice by everyone before embarking on endeavor or projects, as it helps to ensure that the person form a good understanding of background, resources, limits, timing and target, that resources are channelled in the right direction, which ironically may serve to lessen the amount of work and chances of failure later on.

Let's use a salesperson to illustrate an example. Tobias, a sales specialist selling IT security solutions based in Germany, is tasked to handle the UK market.

Before he jumped into sales, there should be planning and preparation involved, and which should be largely market focused.

Background- strength of the product, how big is the market, what are the trends in the market, what is the overall size of the addressable market, who are the competitors, any regulatory and compliance concerns, how will Brexit affect the market.

Resources- how much time does he have, how much budget can he spend on marketing collaterals.

Limits- budgetary constraints, customer objections, competitors price wars, and how Brexit again will limit the sales activities.

Timing- Is it a good time to sell, how will Brexit again affect the activities, should he aim for periods before it happens.

Target- relevant stakeholders or key opinion leaders within UK, most highly valued leads.

Right Channel in Right Direction- all of the above, with consideration for the largest amount of Return of Investment (ROI), in the most efficient and cost saving manner.

Your job function may not be similar to Tobias' but the premises are basically the same. Taking into account those points that were mentioned, it is important to know what you are doing (background), know how much you can do (resources), know how much you can't do (limits), know when you should execute the plans (timing), if you have correctly executed the work at the right area (targets).

Planning ahead is all encompassing in many aspects in life, and can be applied likewise to your interactions with colleagues, before meetings, writing reports, and even answering emails. In a way, reading this book can also be considered as some kind of planning and preparation for the employee to have a higher chance of securing a good outcome in their career.

The Measure of Work

Joseph and Justin were sales executive, contributing similar functions to the sales team; clinching new accounts and closing sales. Joseph was a superstar in the team, closing many accounts and clinching many deals. Justin did not manage to close as many accounts as Joseph but he focused his efforts on the few accounts to grow them, devising strategies to increase sales revenue from each of them.

While Joseph closed many accounts, after a year, it was reviewed that the many accounts were giving problems to the company, with delayed payments and not meeting sales targets, whereas Justin managed to get the few accounts to secure high growth. Naturally in the course of succession plans, Justin was slated to be the sales manager, whereas Joseph was given a business development role to support Justin, to his dismay. It is not too hard to guess where Joseph did wrong and what strengths were recognized in Justin.

As you can see here, at the end of the day, the company always looks at the revenue. I had mentioned before in "What the Companies Really Care About", the utmost priority is "Positive Numbers". When we compared the two sales persons, Joseph, while managing to expand market and closing many accounts, did not manage to secure as much revenue for the company as Justin. Justin on the other hand also demonstrated the quality of "Smooth Operations"- he manage those few accounts really well, getting them to hit targets and not contributing to problems- not bringing extra work to the team to take care of problems. In this case here, we see that Justin is aptly suitable for sales management, whereas Joseph's strength primarily only lie in expanding the market. When we look into the "Measure of Work", we also have to consider the functions of the hired positions.

While we had discussed examples of sales and commercial functions, there are different measures respective to the different types of functions. Other types, like accountants- their measure of work is primarily about balancing the spreadsheets and studying accounting data, ensuring the entries and transactions are accurate, and thereafter compile and analyze them. Their key value to the company is to ensure "Smooth Operations", that their meticulous work will ensure the finances are calculated and thereafter projected accordingly.

As one performs the Daily Grind, the employee should consciously ensure that their daily work will be contributive to their overall function, and only when one can perform the delegated function well, are there any rooms for negotiating other types of work done. Because when one cannot even perform their function well, the management will usually not be too keen to delegate additional tasks to such an employee.

Advice for the Mediocre Employee

What if you are not as good as you want to be? You'd have noticed that many entries in the books are about dealing with mediocre bosses and employees; but what if you are one of them? Fret not, you may have unknowingly set yourself up towards probable success.

When one gets into the essence of the strategies; you would find out that I am actually advocating the readers to assume an image of (false) modesty, an understated impression of relative inferiority in relation to the bosses and co-workers. This 'relative inferiority' is not a sign of weakness or lack of competency, but a psychological tactic to lower the guard of people, to assuage their inner insecurities and competitiveness.

The image can be adopted by someone who has exemplary qualities, or someone without, because personal talents are not the key; it is really about situational awareness, reticence and adaptability. When one begins as a mediocre employee, chances are his or her outlook and work contributions have already conveyed such an impression.

For the mediocre employee, he or she has set a baseline to others with regard to his or her work; but make sure this mediocrity does not falter below to sheer incompetency- that is a dangerous signal with more cause for concern.

The mediocre employee who hovers at the baseline creates lowered expectations for the immediate supervisor or surrounding colleagues. They will see this person as just another drone in the office, and probably don't feel threatened as long as the work function is fulfilled.

But when we rationalize the bottom, it is apparent that there will be plenty of room for tremendous upsides. Any slight improvements will be perceived as exponential. A mediocre employee who is conscious about his or her weakness can utilize this fact to contemplate the furthering of career, taking advantage of opportunities to unleash "The Kairotic Moment" to raise his or her status to greater heights.

It is no secret that many of the people in senior management are some of the most mediocre ones in existence.

Making Exact Promises And Delivery

There is no real advantage in overpromising. You are setting unreasonable bar to both yourself, and the other party (be it boss, client, etc). When the outcome falls short of expectations, you will be held responsible for setting such expectations, and as a result, the failure to deliver will diminish your capability, credibility and value to the other party. In all engagements, it is not appropriate to set the expectations too high. However, it is also not wise to set too low an expectation.

While the world is sold on popular business truisms, the world is not necessarily getting any better. Such oft-repeated quotes like 'Underpromise and Overdeliver' has in reality very little success stories in work and business, except in lining the pockets of the so called self-improvement gurus.

We are all informed on the dangerous ill effects of 'Overpromise and Underdeliver', but the reverse can be equally dangerous. Let's dissect the golden mantra of 'Underpromise and Overdeliver' and see what we will arrive at.

Going above and beyond a promise does not elucidate real value proposition. When a client (or a boss) make demands, this expectation is pegged to a higher value projection. The employee or provider who suggests or reciprocates this value expectation with a proposition below the value projections, creates a pocket of 'negotiated offset' which falls short of expectations initially, and will begin informing the subconscious of the other party of 'hedging' from this person.

If the supply (or results) far exceeds the expectation with the 'negotiated offset', this informs the subconscious that their 'hedging' hypothesis of the employee or provider is proven true, and raises the doubt perception from the other party.

In corporate terms, this is viewed upon as 'sandbagging', which implies that the employee is hiding true amount of opportunities during reporting to management, and thereafter outperforming the numbers that are reported, which brings about distrust from the management.

In pure retail analogy, imagine that you wanted a bottle of vitamin at the pharmacy. The retailer promises you a discount from the standard retail price of the vitamin. After you have paid at the counter, the retailer gives you another bottle of vitamin supplement for free. Contemplate this and see if you think that you've stumbled upon an excellent deal, or if you feel something dodgy about the vitamin supplement or the pharmacy.

The key to successful promises and delivery is to foster the perception of trust. When demands are made with the expectation pegged to a higher value projection, make an effort to show to the other party that you will try to aim within what has been projected to you; not aiming higher or lower than what is mentioned. Or if you are the proponent, propose exactly what you think you can deliver. When you deliver, provide the same valued product and/or services that was expected of you. The other party will think that they are getting the value of the product/service AS WELL AS the effort from you to meet their expectations, and for that, it is much appreciated.

There is no 'negotiated offset', therefore no notion of 'hedging' and therefore cast little to no doubt when the exact request or proposition has been met with exact delivery. And thus ensuring continued trust in the business or work relationship.

Make No Claims

Previously, we have discussed about promises and delivery, but that should only happen in obligatory situations (when asked). When possible, a wise employee should never ever make claims about anything, especially when he or she is not confident on delivering the results. One of the key catalysts of poor work reputation are based on inflated claims which never materialize.

People are instantly judged when claims do not lead to corresponding results. While it can bring about certain embarrassment, on a more serious note, it creates doubt, disappointment, disdain and reduction in confidence in the other party. In the office, it may also serve as ammunition for detractors and opponents, who will gladly gloat at the failure and mock this person's capability.

A failed claimant will be seen as someone who bites off more than he or she can chew, a talk big, a sad joke, an unreliable person who is too eager to impress than having any real competency, proficiency or capability. An employee who suffers from this may become an object of ridicule for a long time, usually finding it hard to redeem him or herself, and may eventually get ostracized, side lined.

If an employee is not confident about the work or project, do not make any claims about success, especially to his or her immediate bosses, who will be placed in higher scrutiny. And even when one is confident, one should never be too cocksure about successes, because there are many factors, some of them unexpected, which may cause even the best planned and executed projects to fail. Do not pop champagnes too early; hold the celebration until good results happen.

Offer Solutions, Not Complaints and Excuses

When problems arise at work, or results fail to meet expectations, the employee may have to be answerable to the bosses, or other co-workers involved in the same project. A person should not lose sleep over it, but accept the fact that this is an inevitable part of working life.

We have to understand that nothing in life is perfect; the best planned and thought out projects can still fail based on many factors, some of which are beyond the control of the employee. With that in mind, it is rather more important to see how the employees handle such situations.

The employees are frequently judged by other co-workers on their work performances. Aside from results, they are also judged on how they handle problems. When faced with scrutiny, criticisms and inquiries, it is definitely not to an employee's advantage when he or she becomes emotional and defensive, because that can be perceived as conceited, insecurity, and desperation.

When I was working for organizations in the past, I have noticed that every employees who try to justify problems and poor results with excuses and complaints tend to get into trouble at some point in their job. Most of the time, the verdict came up with the person being somewhere along the line of unprofessional, and usually the executions are the doings of the bosses.

What good are complaints and excuses? They are annoying, regressive, and do not serve to resolve any problems, than to further fuel the stress situation. Instead of more annoyance and stress, what the bosses would like to hear are rather solutions to the problems.

Even when the employees do not have the best solutions to the problems, at least any effort to be remediative is still more welcoming than complaints and excuses. When an employee gives solutions, especially when they are effective ones, the person will be seen as resourceful, conscientious, having fortitude and quite capable. The solutions will also lessen headaches and offer reliefs for the bosses, who were probably also quite frustrated and stressed out by the problem, aside from the many other problems they also likely face frequently.

Attempt Assigned Tasks

One of the bosses' greatest pet peeves are employees who do not attempt assigned tasks. No matter how close and amicable are the relationships between the boss and the subordinate, it will be placed in jeopardy when the employees cannot or does not want to fulfil a given task, especially when it is directly requested by the boss. Do note the subtext. When I mentioned 'attempt assigned tasks', it does not mean 'finish assigned tasks'. I will get to that later.

Sure, there are times when a person's plate is too full, or when the given tasks are too difficult to be finished in a timely manner, but the least that the employee can do is at least attempt to follow up with updates. All visible evidence of efforts are still appreciated, regardless of whether the task can be properly completed or not.

Because when there are perceived lack of work or urgency to do the task, the first instinct of the boss is to start worrying about his or her authority over the subordinate. Insubordination is also treated seriously in the books of most companies' policies, and if the boss is not agreeable to begin with, this can be a good excuse to get rid of the subordinate.

Secondly, the boss may likely panic over the effect a stalled or ignored task can do to the rest of the work, as this may potentially hijack the function.

In order to not err on the side of trouble, every tasks which are reasonable and legit within the function's framework should have some form of updates. Especially the ones that are personally tasked by the immediate superior.

In order to keep track of the work that needs to be done, one useful suggestion is to have one source of tracking: either one notebook which details the dates and to-do-lists, or set up a task pane on an email browser with notifications and reminders.

Do also continue to finish assigned tasks when appropriate, but do take caution at tasks which might affect job sustainability. There are some tasks which should not be completed, because once they are completed, the person is not rendered useful anymore. Such jobs are usually project or contract based jobs, or those types which may contribute to a situation whereby the completion of the task can result in redundancy of further involvement.

I will illustrate one example here. Anthony was hired by a small company to come up with systemizing marketing processes as well as implementation of the CRM. Knowing well the history of the company, Anthony understood that this company never had the intention of having a marketing or operations unit in the first place. He knew that he was hired to set up a system, and will surely be made redundant afterwards. He needed to stay at least one year in the job to have credibility on his resume, so he timed his work to ensure that it will not be completed until one year of his stay, because it may lead to premature retrenchment.

Always Have Contingency

Nobody wants to end up scrambling for help when problem arises. In order to avoid those scenarios, it is always good to have a backup plan. And this can only happen when the employee has the good habit to always prepare contingency for every situations, should things head south.

It can begin with a backup for all work done, the documents made in the laptop. Depending on the IT policies specific to the company; an employee may or may not be able to save the files separately into a separate storage device; but most companies would have some internal cloud storage for such purposes if they are not happy with information saved elsewhere. Or when one is working on a document, it is always helpful to have several copies saved, in case the file gets corrupted (which can actually happen from time to time). Corporate laptops can also break down from time to time, and having backups will save a person from having all work hijacked by technological failure.

The employee should also have some Plan Bs, or even Cs or Ds for works and/or projects in the event of failure or mistakes, which may happen, especially if they are beyond the control of the person. If it is a client which an employee is working on, he or she should always secure other clients to turn to if the dealings do not turn out well. If an employee is making a proposal to the management, he or she should always have some ways to handle objections and offer alternatives should initial ideas get rejected. Before the employee even talk to the more senior people in the company, he or she needs to have a series of answers handy should the conversation gets tough.

On a more macro level, the employee should even has contingency plan for their own career, on a short or long term basis. Every employee should always expect the worst to happen in the company, like retrenchment, and therefore should **always be on the lookout for career opportunities** even when everything seems to turn out well during the employment or tenure. Because if the employee gets booted out of the company, especially when it is a sudden one, he or she will be able to tide over with sufficient preparations.

Keeping a Paper Trail

Or emails, documents trail where applicable. This is a good practice which every employee should attempt to do, for it will definitely come in handy at some point, especially during contentious situations.

A paper trail by definition means a series of documents providing written evidence of a sequence of events or the activities of a person or organization.

It can serve as a time capsule capturing past events, which can be used for a variety of purposes. It is also something which can be recognized and considered in the corporate world, because the evidences are tangible, worthy of examination than say hear say accounts.

On a work basis, the paper trail is useful to serve as reminder, or reference. It can also be a way to track progress for projects and goal setting. Beginning with email threads, or documents which are properly saved, they should be easily retrievable to the user, to make finding them more convenient for effective usage.

Often in work, the employee might come across amnesiac bosses or colleagues who forgot or rescinded on what they had said before, especially instructions or tasks. One useful application on the paper trail is that it can archive those conversations. Always make it a point for co-workers or customers to send email confirmations, than to do it verbally; at the end of the day, only the black and white can be used.

In more contentious situations, the paper trail may serve as evidence to prove a point or case, potentially protecting the employee in the process, assuming that the past evidences are to his or her advantage.

Emails- Delay Replying, Check for Mistakes

Every employee would have at some point regretted the emails that were sent; either for the mistakes conveyed within the email or directed to the wrong recipients. At best, the employee would have been deemed careless and reactive. At worst, serious mistakes can cost job and reputation.

In reaction to such cases, urgent contingency like mail recalls or follow-ups have been proven to be tremendously embarrassing and ineffective. Mail recalls for that matter never seem to work; because it is a non-function for recipients who check their email on mobile devices, and that it is a messy approach which leaves notification even if it manages to work. And follow-up emails are pathetic, desperate and can raise red flags to the potential employer. Hence, the best safeguard measure is to always delay in replying and recheck the emails for mistakes.

In the corporate environment, sometimes it pays to procrastinate on replying or even not to reply at all to avoid costly mistakes. It is good practice to construct the email without adding any of the recipient addresses, and have it saved as draft. When a draft is finished, repeatedly check on the contents (grammatical ones are actually of the least concerns) for intent, phrasing and especially numbers if you are reporting up figures. Then ponder for a while to see where this email should rightfully go to, before proceeding to add the recipients. Unless you are sending a neutral email, it is usually unwise to include recipients in the bcc, because once again, mobile devices somehow gets around it and sometimes reveal the recipients in the bcc (this is especially dangerous when you are snitching on someone to the boss).

Make it a habit to create drafts, review drafts, and cautiously select the email recipients for every email that you want to write. If something urgent comes along, it doesn't hurt to drop a short and safe note to delay (e.g. I will get back to you later) the process. Try to reduce the rates of regretful emails sent, and continually upkeep the impression that you are thoughtful, careful and reliable.

Emails- Concise, Clear and Instructive

Effective communications happen when messages are conveyed clearly, concisely and instructively. Clarity ensures that the intended message is intelligible and clear to understand. Concise information is catered to further convey the points with relevance and within context. Instructive communications package the information to follow logical flow, is process-driven and in easy-to-follow layout. Sometimes we see people get carried away in writing long essays in simple requests and reports.

The long paragraphs, flowery prose and intellectual analysis are great for novels and theses but are not appreciated by the recipients who just try to read the message and get the job done. Beside emails, such long essays also do not find fans in marketing messages, social media, collaterals and other medium.

It is recommended that the sentences are kept short with relevant points. If possible, highlight important notes in point forms, or literally highlight the texts with color (except red). Of course try not to make messages too terse in emails because it may come across as rude or lackadaisical; this hyper short style works better in WhatsApp or SMSes. Also, in email writing, try to put the key points of the messages into the titles so the recipients know what they are expecting. When our messages are clear, concise and instructive, it plants the subliminal impression to the other party that we are thoughtful, empathetic and systematic.

Respecting the Co-worker's Personal Limits

No, it's not about bullying, harassing or insulting fellow co-workers. They are so obviously serious, there's no point talking about them. What I am going to discuss here is about how certain work habits may go overboard and infringe on the personal time, and tolerance of the co-workers, making them unhappy. There are some things which are perhaps not so obvious when one is caught up with performing certain work function, but care must be taken, no matter how small or insignificant they can be.

I spoke earlier about emails. Now, we can use an email example to illustrate the point here. And it is about sending emails or contacting colleagues at improper time.

This has to be considered also with regard to what is the usual practice of the companies and different cultural context which may be specific to certain regions, but generally most western companies tend to want to not disturb their employees after work hours, weekends and when the employees are on leaves or vacations by sending out specific emails or calling them.

That means, if you have the habit of sending emails during midnight, calling your colleagues during dinner time, or doing the same when they are enjoying their time off in the

Caribbean, you should be mindful that it is a sign of disrespect to this employee. Surely, some of them will respond, but it tends to leave a bitter aftertaste, and they will not tend to like you that much, or try to avoid you next time.

Another point which I want to talk about here is with regard to respecting the limits, the threshold, the tolerance an employee has. Assuming that this person is your subordinate or peer, he or she can only take so much requests or pressure from you if they are tasked, or asked for help. If one senses that the person's plate is full, or is on the verge of a breakdown, one should not push his or her luck to make the person do more, by being too pushy, aggressive, or barky, as it can potentially be the straw that will break the camel's back.

Unfortunately, some things can only get done when someone is pushing for it, and if you have no choice but to do it, then do it cautiously measured, and do not press the button to cause the other party to go berserk.

Nobody likes a pushy slave-driver, and this will tend to reflect badly on your professional image, even though your intention is good, for the path to hell is paved with good intentions. The highly distressed party may harbor great resentment and vendetta or worse, stomp off to the nearest human resources office with extreme distress signals (crying) and a likelihood to exaggerate the incident.

Ask for Help When Needed

No man is an island, and not especially in the office. No matter how competent a person is, it is impossible to accomplish everything alone.

The very nature of the employee's job function is likely already tied to other functions, either as a receiver or provider of support. And even within the same function, it is useful to be able to get support from fellow colleagues who are more experienced. In order to thrive well, or even simply to execute a task, the employee needs to be able to get help when needed, because that can become a determinant for accomplishment of that certain task. The only thing is if help can be so readily available.

I have discussed before about how one should appear helpful (in 'Cultivating the Right Image') and yet being selective about helping ('Restrict Helpfulness'). The two opposing rules are fine lines to tread carefully; yet, we are all aware that help is something that has a certain condition of reciprocity- a person will tend to get help if he or she is helpful to begin with. However, we should look at the nuance of the two opposing rules and see how they can meet.

One should appear helpful- as the phrasing suggests, that is an image of helpfulness only. Being selective about helping- that is a strategy which focuses on not setting precedence in letting colleagues habitually impose one on thankless tasks, but rather to be selective about helping. The two rules can be essentially similar: it is all pretence, conservation of resources and tactical dynamics. It certainly takes some finesse to balance helpfulness and build the necessary rapport.

Nevertheless, do always ask for help when needed, even if you are not the most helpful person in the company. At some point, even the most unwilling colleagues have to oblige, especially if it is his or her duty to do so; no one likes to be blamed as the culprit for being the cause of any specific functions to fail in the company.

Be Consistent

Many would have thought that all people like surprises. But if the target is the boss, it may not always be the case.

Most bosses actually do not want to have too many surprises even if they carry good news, unless they have something to do with a turnaround of a bad situation that both the boss and the employee are facing. Positive surprises are only a nicer version of shock; they cannot be anticipated by the other party, and hence may imply lack of control from themselves, unpredictability of the employee, and will potentially throw the other party off balance.

Of course, some nice surprises every now and then are fine, but if one does it frequently, it will make the bosses very wary and insecure about the person.

Do not be fooled into thinking that sudden upwards spike in performance or massive successes are something which can guarantee career success to the employee within an organization. Such sudden or unexpected movements seldom impress the superior, but are more likely to make them rethink the danger of having this employee around, for they are disruptive to business projections that had already been forecasted, and this person also has the likelihood of bettering the immediate superior.

Rather, the best strategy for the employee is to maintain consistency in most part of their work, especially early into the job. I had mentioned in "Time Your Performance" under the "The Art of Concealment" that it is unwise to show hands too early. If you are planning to surprise some people with a defining moment in your career history, make sure that it is targeted during the right time period to the right audience. The immediate bosses are usually not the right audience, but rather the bosses of the boss who would be appropriate.

By consistent work, it means having results which are predictable and expected to the immediate bosses. Surely there will be peaks and troughs throughout the period, but try hard to keep them on a median, with allowance for 'organic growth' during a time period at a reasonable percentage and rate. By keeping consistent work, it will make the bosses and co-workers more comfortable around this employee, because the consistency this person brings fosters trust, reliability and confidence.

The Kairotic Moment

Definition of Kairos: a time when conditions are right for the accomplishment of a crucial action;   the opportune and decisive moment.

This is a reverse of the previous rule, "Be Consistent". And we have also discussed similar concepts during 'Time Your Performance' under the chapter "The Art of Concealment". A Kairotic Moment is that momentous time for one to act, to showcase the true prowess, talent, competency, which had been hidden from sight for the longest time in the company.

The employee who had followed the earlier rules stated in the book, understood the importance of keeping the cards close to the chest, to blend into the office crowd like everyone else, while keenly observing and learning about the culture, the people and functions of the office, always consistent or work and behavior. The periods of stoic reticence will temper and sharpen the sword to be unleashed at the Kairos moment, when the time, place and situation are triangulated, giving a clear signal to act.

Some examples of such Kairos moment are: when the employee finally has the opportunity to perform in the presence of the bosses of the boss; when the company undergoes a crisis and is in need of a miraculous recovery;

when the company decides to start pitting employees against one another to compare who has the most value.

When such opportunities are presented, the employee should give in all the best to strike, as there is a good chance that it will enable one to get elevated to the next status in the job, when the attempts are successful. This strategy of course is not for every readers; it is only meant for the ambitious employee who wants to get ahead in the job. There are certainly some risks associated with this endeavor, but I have laid down some strategies later in the book to enable a higher probability of success.

6. Realpolitik

Realpolitik is a German word which translates to "actual politics'. It is politics or diplomacy based primarily on considerations of given circumstances and factors, rather than explicit ideological notions or moral and ethical premises. The politics which take place in the company and/or the office is pretty much realpolitik at work.

Politics and realpolitik are dirty words. I know many people who would immediately say, "politics is not my stuff", to distance themselves from such associations, as well as any allusions to Machiavellianism, because these are ultimately thought of as evil. Yet politics is actually an inherent nature of human beings, even though most don't see themselves as a practitioner or has no interest in it. What they do not understand is that it is pervasive in every aspects of life, often taking place subconsciously: e.g. when a child runs crying to his mother for support after fighting with his older brother, he is already engaging in some type of politics.

Politics is defined as activities aimed at increasing status or power. Country leaders are politicians because they aimed at governance or area from other parties or countries. The child who runs to the mother for support is aiming at backing to increase power to deal with the stronger brother.

Some of the root causes for politicking are: a) humans are social animals, b) humans observe hierarchy, c) humans are divisive, d) and humans are primarily selfish and want power and benefits. The working world- consisting of corporations and companies, unfortunately, is one of the places that are festering with the most political people. Because these places are populated with people from all walks of life, to contend for opportunities and resources; from the nooks and crannies of the office, to the directors in the boardroom, people with different personalities, ambitions, and preferences.

At a higher level, the company faces two opposing forces, which were discussed in "Knowledge and Propriety". These forces contend at the differences in fundamental values which the employees identify with. At a more intrinsic level, it is about career ambitions, alignment and attainment of power. People of similar views on the three things above tend to group together. At a more micro level, it could generally be about preferences/differences, backgrounds, personalities, work styles, and also prior disagreements when work is concerned. Within the same chapter in "Knowledge and Propriety" I also discussed tools which enable one to find out political factions, so that one will get a good idea about the different dynamics within the company.

The whole point of political play in the company is to utilize the backing and power of groups to achieve specific goals. While it can be individualized, one man army is generally not a common and effective route. It always certainly involves people who got together by convenience and necessity, and relies on the camaraderie, the relationships and consensual agreement to follow the larger direction of these groups, to execute and realize plans, to crush political opponents and make its political mark with the consolidated power.

Over time, old or existing political groups can be further fragmented into smaller factions, members can move out to join other groups or form new groups, as priorities change accordingly to different circumstances and differences in personality from within the groups- goals will also change, coupled with personal motivations deemed fit. The course of politics is always dynamic and mutable, with no long term political fixture and no long term allies and enemies. An unwilling employee may even have no choice but gets pulled into the political whirlpool; a person who wants to maintain neutrality will usually turn into a punching bag for the political factions from all sides, especially when company gets into extremely contentious situations.

On the other hand, the choices of aligning to a political group may determine the fate of the person in the company. When a person is not careful, he or she may fall into the wrong side of politics and suffer the consequences. If the person is on the winning side, it may be that one thing which will propel one to greater heights, leveraging on the effectiveness of group power in this constant game of hegemony.

All of these may sound scary, but it is the reality of the working world and it may have already happened at your workplace, otherwise you wouldn't be reading this book. At this point, if you just want to do your job and stay out of trouble, do not read on. Otherwise, enjoy.

First, Get Along with The Boss and Team

Before one even entertain any political notion, there are some basic precursors which first needs to be taken care of, and that is- **getting along with the boss and the team**. If the employee has no ability to even get along with the own boss and team, it is impossible for this person to go anywhere else in the company.

To get along with the boss and team, it is simply about not stepping on their toes, and just getting by and getting your work done without constant threats, disagreements and ill will- just a normal day in the office where you don't get bothered by dramas. There is no need to be buddies with them, but there is nothing stopping you. In order to get along with them, the person just needs to be agreeable (amicable and cooperative) and work functional (do the job relatively well). And when there are disagreements, the wise employee should do best to be conciliatory.

When one is assigned into a team structure, there is nothing much the person can do except to learn best to fit and adjust. An employee who is not well adjusted with the boss and the team could face the dangerous possibility of getting turned against by own team members, which is not pleasant, because the person will suffer and not be able to get out of the situation easily. It is a tormenting experience to harbor ill will and yet having to face the colleagues everyday in the same office. In order to even get by, the employee constantly needs to have a good set of tactics in dealing with the boss and team members. There are several tools discussed earlier in the book which might help the person (many of them covered under "Knowledge and Propriety").

A general rule of thumb is to adapt and be conciliatory. Sometimes, a person may need to compromise. Keep your ego down until it is the right time to exercise your prowess. If the boss is really bad, one may be able to find comfort with the colleagues. Or vice versa. Understandably, it may get to a point whereby it is just too tedious to even get along with the boss and the team, but if it happens in the outset, the employee should do well to leave this job early before things get worse. If that is not an option, one might have to suffer injustice and suck it up, while waiting for an opportunity to alleviate this misery, when there are changes to the company structure, or when one manages to secure a job elsewhere.

The very basics that is required of you, to reiterate, is to first get along with the boss and colleagues. Everything else is secondary.

Assuming you have succeeded in getting along with the boss and the team, you can then start to plan your next moves. Look beyond them and keep your eyes open for political options. When the basics are set in foundation, it is possible to prepare your flight towards greater heights.

The Merits of Diplomacy

Most people probably remembered Otto von Bismarck more for his "Blood and Iron" quote and the image of a war hawk, but little did they know that he was one of the most brilliant diplomat and statesman who had skilfully used balance of power diplomacy to maintain united Germany's position in a peaceful Europe. Pure belligerence itself would not ensure Germany's success in the modern world. It involves complex and intricate diplomacy at work which is of greater importance.

Diplomacy at a higher level is about managing international relationships. When it comes to day to day interactions, it is defined as the art of dealing with people in a sensitive and tactful way. It is a fallacy to assume that the leaders in the company get to where they are now by sheer bullying and elbowing their way to the top. And, even if some of them do behave like aggressive bulldogs, they probably only do it to the underlings, and not to the senior people who matters. The further one goes up in rank, the more diplomacy is at play.

When the employee can, he or she should always cultivate diplomacy. In order to do so, the first thing that should be done is to keep the ego in check. Ego and self esteem are the culprits and causes of the downfall of many potentially great talents. In order to thrive in a company, a person should always be adaptable (which I stressed on in "The Key to

Survival") to people and situations, and frequently it involves foregoing of ego and even making compromises and suffering short term injustices, in preparation for long term goals. A reactionary person may win the battles and lose the war- one may be able to get back at an opponent by retaliating with forceful words, but in the long term, he or she may be condemned by the rest of the company for such uncouth and unprofessional behavior.

Diplomacy is not just about being nice and amicable to the bosses and co-workers; it is more so, about having the knowledge ("Knowledge and Propriety") to be discrete ("The Art of Concealment"), and congenial ("Projecting the Right Image") to be flexible to situations ("The Key to Survival") in interactions with people and situations.

It is a soft power which is never offensive, but more pervasive, influential and potentially deadlier than brute force and might. Because it aims at the heart of people.

Opportunities in Crisis

The faint-hearted probably would not have gotten this far. They will also likely panic, cower under cover and start toeing the line at the first sight of danger in the company or in their team. In crisis, there will definitely be casualties. But those who harbor big ambitions and dare, will revel at the moments of chaos; because they understand very well that- "The Future Belongs to the Brave" and "Who Dares Win".

Why are crises mightily anticipated? Because it has a very strong element of **change**. When a company, or department gets into a dangerous situation, it will usually take drastic measures and start making big changes within the organization, like restructuring, hires and fires. It is precisely due to this, that those in wait can start to act on and execute their plans. Because there will usually be a change of leaderships, opening up of new positions, and are a great catalyst to upset the previously 'unshaken' status quo (especially if it consists of a mass of mediocre long term fixture), which can be hard to be affected during peacetime.

Within the book, there are a good amount of chapters and topics dedicated to the 'defensives'. Those 'defensives', like observing the rules, hiding and concealing intentions, projecting appropriate images, doing the job well, are what every employee should keep in mind and practice during peacetimes. During peacetimes, the employee may have been subjected to much stoicism in the process and building a fortitude of resilience, resolve, and resources. While carefully observing and behaving, the ambitious employee would have also planned his or her moves preparations for the "Kairotic Moments", which I had discussed as a last topic in "The Daily Grind".

When we move into this chapter, we are turning the tone from 'defensives' to more 'offensives', paying attention to the political subtleties and dynamics which are forming up while drawing up strategies which are pro-active. The more ambitious employee would have started approaching his or her political allies, joining or forming political factions, and awaiting for opportunities to act. There are of course also opportunities which may not always be presented as crises, and there is no stopping the reader to act out and execute political goals when they happen, but the crisis itself presents some of the best opportunities.

Most of the time, the employees may frequently encounter "small crises" than large epic ones involving overall company restructuring. They may come in forms of a team under scrutiny for poor performances, rush to manage bottom lines before the financial year end, and gap filling exercises for missed targets. These can be 'dangerous' enough, and may sometimes lead to one or two fires, and 'opportunistic' enough, leading to one or two accolades. Whenever any of such opportunities present themselves, look at the political positioning, your political affinities, and the potential conflict points and see if it is worth the execution or escalations.

Do Not Stay Neutral For Long

Most employees just want to be left alone and focus on doing their work and getting their monthly pay checks. Work is already hard enough, nobody likes to be perturbed further by the nuisance and nonsense from the politicking colleagues. There is definitely wisdom with being conflict avoidant, minding one's own business and not getting entangled in the political drivel. If only life is that easy.

Many self-help books and career consultants out there always stress on the importance of staying neutral. This is not a wrong advice, but it needs to be updated. The employees should stay neutral whenever they begin in a company; and not eagerly subscribing themselves to the factions. It comes with many good reasons:

a) Newcomers who gets political too fast tend to attract the wrong attention and bad reputation. It is best to maintain a low profile and keep the head down.

b) A person who is relatively new to a company is not well equipped to make sound judgement on the politics taking place.

c) It is always better to observe carefully- the profiles of the co-workers, the dynamics of the political factions, and how they are playing out- who are the current winners and losers.

d) Make assessments of the observations and decide how they affect oneself, are they in line with the values, will they serve to benefit in the short and long term?

However, there may come a time when staying neutral is a difficult option, or even not an option anymore. As the employee stays longer in the company, perhaps given more job responsibilities and seniority, he or she cannot pull the same neutral card anymore. The reasons are:

a) A neutral employee with a certain amount of experience and seniority in the company will be affected by the political drama from the senior management. Almost every senior management has some level of participation in politics, and they will deliberately or subtly seek alliance.

b) The neutral employee, who is not allied to any of the political factions established as part of the senior management game will be sidelined if one party emerge the winner, thereby affecting his or her chance of further career development.

c) The neutral employee will be frequently doubted and suspected as being even more political in nature than the counterparts even when it is not the case, because he or she may be perceived to appear 'neutral' as a front: be it hiding something, harboring secret ambitions, or may be secretly allied to one faction.

d) The neutral employee can be treated as punching bags, or pushovers, to take blame and be the fall guy by the warring factions.

e) When problem comes to the neutral employee (and it can even come from other people, because no matter how neutral or nice a person is, there will always be detractors), he or she may not be able to receive help from those in the political factions, and the problems can get aggravated by the fact that he or she is vulnerable because of lack of backings.

From the instances above, it seems like going neutral may not be the most viable option in the long run, especially if the person has an ounce of ambition. Every men and women who attain great heights are largely able to do so with the assistance and support of allies, patrons, and backers; if it involves friendly forces, it definitely and inevitably involves politics.

Displays of Power Tripping

The Alphas want to be known. The Betas want to imitate. Basically insecure humans like to pull power trips to increase their image of power and to intimidate people. There is usually a psychological element behind those displays, and they can be either subtle and subliminal or explicit and offensive, with the intention of informing the other party, to assert their power and influence. Be familiar with them, it is useful to know.

Power trip displays can either be a habitual display of an individual, or it can deliberately targeted to the colleagues, especially towards subordinates and rivals. Here are some examples of the most frequent power moves which people pull from time to time:

1. **Silence**- This is probably the most powerful amongst the power moves, because it is effective, not abusive, not unprofessional, and it tends to be open-ended. Silence is golden, but also very lethal. If you've seen two persons getting into quarrels, and one of them decides to go silent, it tends to rile the other party up into heightened frustrations, especially if this person tries to press on issue to no avail and response.

At the workplace, this is frequently observed during meetings, when there are disagreements and which tends to end in an uncomfortable aftermath should one party suddenly go silent.

The silent party will usually receive an immense amplification of power, as the one who calls the authority and control, over the other party.

2. **Non Response**- This is almost similar to silence, except that it can take place outside of verbal discussions. Non response is most frequently seen in email conversations, whereby an email is not replied during an expected time, or even indefinitely.

This power move subtly suggests that "I have no time for your crap", and it is usually pulled by more senior members of the company on the rest of the underlings. This power move however is not advisable to be used by a subordinate to the boss, as it may either be treated as a case of negligence or insubordination.

3. **Clearing of Throat**- Throughout my many years in the corporations, I had seen so many examples of employees pulling this little trick, especially towards rivals or people they wanted to intimidate. The less sensitive might be inclined to believe that there were bouts of throat infection outbreak in the offices. The clearing of throats takes place as soon as another person is in close proximity, or during brief encounters. It draws attention, and the undertone implies authority, warning, or displeasure towards the target.

4. **Curt Replies**- These are actual words which people use to convey an image of superiority, or to express dismissal. When one party starts speaking proper sentences to the other party, and all the other party can reply is, "Good", "Hmm",

"OK", in a curt manner (and with an unimpressed look on the face), there is usually some possibility that the other party is trying to use the "Curt Replies" power move on the talking party. Or it may be so deeply inculcated, it forms the habit of this person to constantly attempt to display his or her authority to every encounter.

5. **Disdainful Questions**- Have you encountered those people who asked you unnecessary questions, after you made some obvious statement, like "I beg your pardon", "I don't understand", or "What do you mean by that"? You may have encountered some pathetic fool who tried to pull a power move on you, by undermining your capability, making you look stupid, incoherent or unintelligible, and thereby increasing his or her superiority over you.

5. **Impatience**- They are trying to act like as if their time is wasted talking to a person, and they have no time for people of lower priority. This display is frequently consisted of several parts, like avoiding the gaze of the other party, pretending to focus elsewhere, looking annoyed or in hurry, and curt replies.

6. **The Psychopathic Pause**- While silence is more of a verbal-related expression, a subtle physical expression can be coupled with it to augment the discomfort to the other party, by having sudden abrupt break during conversations, the glare fixed at either the person or a space with angry intensity, with no other movements. After the pause, for a short, but uncomfortable period of time, normalcy is restored as if nothing happened. This should unsettle the other party enough to not mess around with the probable "psycho".

Be Seen on the Boss's Side

You are informed about how one should not stay neutral for long, but now let's look at things from another perspective- in reality the political clock had already started ticking when the person started the first day of work, reporting to the immediate boss.

Whether the person likes it or not, the immediate boss will serve as the first political ally, by necessity and convenience. The boss's duty is to take care of the subordinate (may not happen) and the subordinate is expected to obey the boss and get work done (these are more certain). Whatever they do, they need to align as a team (or a gang), even when it comes to conflict with other people/departments. The boss usually will not explicitly state so, but would really prefer the employee to stand on his or her side.

To be on the side of the boss doesn't mean that the employee should therefore submit their life to the boss. It is just a political image, and it can change when the time is right. It doesn't equate one turning into a henchman to 'fix' the opposing party. Rather, small safe gestures can be displayed to create a sense of 'loyalty' to the boss and the other co-workers alike. For example, if the boss is negatively questioned by a party, it is always appropriate to jump to the boss's defense with some rebuttals to justify the boss's action while subtly highlighting the quality of the boss. Or when the boss deliberately stayed away from a certain rival group, the subordinate can do the same and not socialize with them.

When the employee is unfortunate enough to draw the short straw with a terrible or fatuous boss, he or she would still need to put up with having this person as the political ally, until help arrives, because the boss is the only line of defense. There is a scenario which allows the reversal of this rule: If abuse (physical or mental ones) is administered by the boss. When you turn the boss to the HR or the political enemies, no one will blame you, because you will be seen as a victim.

If things are not extremely bad, there are valid reasons as to why the wise employee should always stand firmly on the bosses' side when the boss is in a contentious situation with other people.

a.) The immediate boss is someone who directly affects the work and appraisal of the employee. The subordinate should generally be in 'agreement' and 'recognize the authority'. So naturally the employee is obliged to be on the bosses' side.

b.) Even if the supervisor is a boss from hell, most of these types may likely change their attitude towards the subordinate after sensing the person's 'loyalty'. That is, if they have that bit of moral conscience and gratitude (which most but not all people possess; and remember if abuse is administered, there is no reason to put up with this person anymore). The employee may stand to gain more favor from this boss as greater level of trust and appreciation is imbued.

c.) You may be in utter disagreement with the boss, and maybe even preferred the other party, but to forsake your boss in support for the other side, is a very ugly gesture which illicit wrath from not just the boss, but also disgust from other people, including the opposing party. Turncoats are often vilified and tend to be regarded as potential backstabber by almost everyone; therefore, not a good position to get into.

d.) You may also choose to remain neutral and not do anything about it. This is a viable strategy to let the boss take the heat and let him or her burn (probably to accelerate the downfall) especially if the boss is a mediocre leader and there are better options (targeting the boss of the boss or other bosses). But this will not turn out to be a sensible choice if the boss wields considerable power and influence. Also, this will not put you in a more favorable position in the boss's books, thus jeopardizing your chance to get ahead with this boss.

e.) Gestures and evidence of support for the bosses creates the impression of loyalty and righteousness. Even if the boss is not popular in the office, the loyal subordinate will be deemed rather highly, and may stand the chance of being sought after by other leaders.

This relationship may persist, but can also end at some point. For those types that persist, the boss and the subordinate are probably well placed in the company and suitably compatible, and there may be already several instances of mutual benefits (e.g. moving up the career ladder together- the boss gets promoted and then promotes the staff).

It may also end on several notes. When the reporting line is changed, the subordinate may need to report to a different boss. Whenever it is permissible, it always looks good if the subordinate continues to be amicable to the former boss, while also conscious that more priority should be focused at the current boss.

On another note, if the boss and the subordinate falls out, the latter should take care not to appear disloyal to the co-workers' eyes, but rather as a victim of circumstances. This may not be too convincing when the subordinate jumped ship to avoid getting pulled down by the Titanic of the boss's downward spiral, but when that happens, the person may not be in the minority.

Misery Loves Company

There are some people within the company you probably can recognize as miserable creatures. That guy who was ostracized because he did his work sloppily and displayed anti-social behavior, or that lady who was unpopular because she brought her dysfunctional personal life to work, frequently bringing and spreading bad vibes to all her fellow co-workers.

Somehow, we also know or heard of some people in the office with "Jesus Christ Complex" who may see the need to step in and make friends with the disenfranchised, to assist them and alleviate their misery. However, most people are mere mortals, ill equipped with the necessary power and capacity, therefore these 'altruistic individuals' may risk high rates of ending up with futile attempts, and worse still, getting sucked into the misery of these folks.

Misery loves company, and it is infectious and contagious. The wretched tends to bring nothing but misery, unlucky vibes and some philosophical afterthoughts. They will definitely and gladly 'outsource' those negative feelings to the willing ears, and would not hesitate to drag the helpful person to their same level. When we consider the utility of them in the schemes of politics within the company, they serve no value and may even potentially hijack and disrupt political plans and even normal work functions. Anyone found associated with them tend to be tarred with the same brush.

Henceforth, stay far away from them, do not touch them with the ten foot pole, and pray that they will improve. Do not feel the compulsion to help, because you may not even be able to help yourselves out of the quagmire when you slipped there.

Misery is a condition which will improve on itself when the time is right. And from what I had observed, it usually involves personal effort than concerted help or interventionist approach. And the impetus for them to improve usually begins when they are inspired.

* If you are one of those people who are susceptible to misery, take your time to brood and wallow in your abject negativity; when you are done, get on with life and start planning small goals and make small victories to pull yourselves out of the swamp. I hope this book and future volumes will prove useful to you one day, getting you into the light, but with a little healthy cynicism.

Following the Wrong God Home

People sometimes make mistakes of judgement. But when it comes to political mistakes, it can be extremely costly. Later in this chapter, I will discuss about "Plan Out Political Positioning", which will get a person to make certain political choices. But what if a wrong choice is made? A political employee may have been banking for the losers all along, and this could lead to undesirable consequences. The key to success is to be on the winning side. If only it could be that easy.

When I first discussed about "Find Out the Political Factions" and in "Knowledge and Propriety", it is about identification of political groups. One of the ways to assess the strengths of the group is to look at "Social and Power Gauges" in the same chapter.

After that, sit back and observe what direction is the company generally heading towards, starting with looking at the qualities forming (based on "Opposing Forces at the Workplace" differentiating "Status Quo" and "New Order") in the company, as well as within the senior management who are helming this.

Next, identify if yourself, the boss and team, and the groups fall into any of the qualities which are aligned to this overarching ethos. Any individuals or teams who are aligned to the qualities have higher chances of thriving and winning, especially if they are also sufficiently powerful.

You may have identified the winning faction out of the losing one, but it does not guarantee you that you will be part of the winning faction, because of several conditions- a) they may be your rivals at work, b) your first political ally rightfully is your boss and team and may be opposed to the winning faction, c) the timing is not right yet to be in that group.

When that happens, the decisive employee may need to review the current situation within his own team or faction, and see if it is possible to allow the winning faction to influence changes within the own team or faction.

This comes at a price- it may upset the current structure within the team, and may potentially cost the job of the boss and co-workers. This is a high risk endeavor, but may be worth taking if: the boss and the co-workers are impeding your progress within the team.

Rather than follow your losing team or faction into the watery graves, start to see if there is potential to leverage on existing "conflict points" (which will be discussed later in the chapter) to remediate existing hostility or rivalry and see if it helps to secure your chance to be the new captain of this ship without jumping ship.

It may have some chances of success, especially when the discontent from the other party is not directed at you, but with your boss and team at large, and if there are meeting of needs.

Most of the time, the average employees would probably not need to go through this because it can be a rather daunting task- but when crisis strikes the company, such moves may see one getting a foothold on the paths to new avenues and opportunities.

As with the title of the topic, "Following the Wrong God Home" is a costly mistake for those one who wants to maintain survival and progression within the company. It is especially piteous to have an exemplary and talented performer to be subjected to stoop to, and stick with the sinking crew of mediocre quality, thus cutting short of this individual's prospects, and worse, even costing his or her job in the organization.

Plan Out Political Positioning

If the reader is relatively comfortable with the boss and the team and the job and does not wish to get involved with something as dirty as politics, it is not recommended to read on from here. However, if there is an ounce of ambition in the bones, then one might find this topic useful.

Let's say that the wise employee has gotten the basics right; managing to stabilize his or her place in a job function and getting by quite OK without unnecessary dramas, but growing restless with being stuck in this one place at the same position- while contemplating to climbing to greater heights within the company. When that happens, the person has been bitten by the ambition bug and may need to start looking at ways to further such goals.

An ambitious employee should know exactly what he or she wants, laying down some short term and long term goals, both inside and outside the organization.

The first place to look at is within the same team. Most progressions take place internally, and you may sometimes get promoted by the boss if you do your job well, but there may be the unfortunate circumstance that the next level which you can go to, probably belong to your boss right now. A more conscientious person will enable both the boss and oneself to progress together, doing work which will help the boss gets promoted, thus getting promoted as well. A more ruthless person may wish the boss to step out or down to make way for succession. Nevertheless, there is also a need to look out for the other colleagues within the team. Are they also as equally or if not more ambitious as you are? Have you identified some potential rivals within the group?

Next, take a step back and see how the boss and the team are perceived in the eyes of the five departments (discussed in "Knowing the Other Departments"). Take one more step back and look at the overall company and its senior leadership. What is their general workstyle (based on "Opposing Forces at the Workplace")?

After making these observations, start to go deeper and ask yourself these questions:

1. **What do you think are the chances that your boss will promote you?** If you are on the way towards promotion, you probably wouldn't bother yourself with trying to figure out a way to get ahead. When the chances are low, one may have to rely on politics.

2. **What direction is the company heading towards and what forces are helming it?** Remember the discussions on "Opposing Forces at the Workplace". Where do you think the company currently fit in right now? Are the Top Dogs also embracing similar qualities?

3. **If changes are taking place in the company, will your boss and team be affected? Are there opposing party against your team?** Compare the general qualities of the company with that of the boss and team. Chances are there might be antithetical groups opposed to your team as well. Study them and see if they can be of use to you any chance later.

4. **What is the strength of your boss and team, and how do you think they can fare in adversities?** Use some tools like "Social and Power Gauges" to tell whether they may be able to weather the storm.

5. **Where are the conflict points?** Remember, in "Find Out the Political Factions", I mentioned about conflict points, which arise from tensions? Identify them and if possible, exploit them to your advantage.

6. **Are there possibilities to secure supporters and backers?** These people should be preferably of considerable power and they can be anyone from within and outside the team. It begins by networking.

7. **What are the necessary steps to take to begin networking with potential supporters and backers?** In order to gain supporters and backers, the person usually need to couch a certain value, either subtly or explicitly of benefit to drive an impetus for the other party to act.

8. **Are there opportunities to strike?** Look out for coming crises (opportunities) and see if a "Kairotic Moment" and/or "Escalation" can be implemented.

9. **If plan fails, do you have a contingency plan?** How to get out of trouble when things go south.

10. **What will it cost you?** If things fail, will it cost you your job or more?

After you have carefully thought out all scenarios in the list, it is possible to see out how you want to proceed with your political plans and positioning, taking careful steps to roll them out gradually. The items in the list constitute one political endeavor, or one cycle; there may be more of such scenarios for one to encounter in the course of the career.

Keeping One's Hands Clean

Before anyone starts acting on the political plans, one should always be mindful of one thing- never get caught with your hands in the cookie jar. Refer to "Protect Your Reputation", and chant it like a mantra. Underhanded moves, dirty deeds and many political exploits are much hated, and are costly when apprehended.

Some people earn the reputation as "Teflon Man"; do not even admire them, for they were already known to always get away with their dirty deeds. Dirty deeds are subjective, but if any plans are political in nature, they are already deemed dirty by many. Be even more skilled than the "Teflon Man"; keep your hands so clean and records so spotless that nobody would assume that you are capable of being devious.

A wise employee understands that all the acts of observing rules and ethical behavior are observed by many. Those impressions count. When political move becomes necessary, make it look legit and always have justifications and alibi. Political rapport should be projected as relationship building. Political undermining should be projected as constructive criticism. And whenever possible, do not get personally involved, but leverage it through someone else.

Benefits of Networking

In order to even find political allies and supporters, it may require a person to be active in networking. Networking is defined as the action or process of interacting with others to exchange information and develop professional or social contacts and it is useful not just in terms of building relationships; it is also a powerful tool to gain information.

Not everyone is predisposed to have such skill sets or energy to keep up with it, especially when one is more introverted, but it can be practiced and focused to make it more expedient. One does not need to begin to expend social energy, seeking out everybody in the organization. It is simply a matter of quality over quantity.

Every networking is somewhat transactional in nature, and the participants will sometimes feel it, but did not consciously give much thoughts about it. When someone made an attempt that seemed blatantly transactional, the person however can instantly come across as insincere and too realistic. The wise employee may find it useful instead, to exercise a more nuanced approach to coat the transactional pursuit with a more personable touch, using some strategies discussed in the next few topics.

Ways to Gain Trust

Trying to gain trust with a colleague is an uphill task in an untrusting place like the office. And in any lousy places within the company, trusts given are usually not complimentary; rather it is a badge for the perceived naivety, and 'safe to handle category' of a trusted person. Nevertheless, the ability to get people to trust you is a highly valued skill, especially when you know yourself as the most untrustworthy person.

In order to gain political supporters, it is important to gain their trust, before one expect them to offer help. It will probably be already quite helpful if one comes across as earnest and sincere. Remember those chapters where I talked about concealing your true self, and projecting images of certain false modesty? The whole point of some of these exercises is to play a sucker to catch the sucker. There is no point in looking clever and cunning when one is in a junior or vulnerable position, it tends not to win support.

One way to draw them in is to give them a perception that they are smarter than you, and that you have certain value which can contribute to their goals and ambitions. Lower their guards by acting forthcoming, giving false confessions (minor things posing no threats to your job) and feigning ignorance/play dumb on things you obviously know. In no time, they will give you a badge of 'safe to handle category'.

Value Propositions

So let's say you're ready to start networking; but who do you target? Review that political plan of yours and see who are likely able to turn up as the potential patron saint to ensure your political success. Do consider some of these questions before talking to the person: a) what do you want to achieve? b) would that person have time for you? c) what do this person want to achieve? d) how is this person in relation to the company, leaders and colleagues, your boss and team; any conflict points? e) what value can you bring them? f) how can they be of help to you?

These questions should clarify exactly what you want, and if the target is qualified. A person is more likely to help you, if you are able to provide the value which will allow the other party to achieve what he or she wants. If this person is of a 'Recipient' (getting support and benefits from either yourself or your team) relationship to you, you're probably off to a good start.

What is the value we are talking about here? This value is largely tied in with needs, and in the work context, are primarily concerned with job security. If you are able to help address those job insecurities of the person, it is half a battle won. It can be anything from expanding their political prowess, means to get back at their rivals, to resolution of long standing work issues, amongst other needs.

Addressing Needs
And Sidestepping Landmines

In order to win genuine support, a person needs to understand the psychology of needs. One who can assuage deep fears and address deep needs of a person is usually successful in having an influence on people.

Every person has different things which can trigger happy, angry or sad emotions, based on what he or she had experienced in life. Across the working world, the most common fear is the lack of job security, and poor financial situation as a result. Many people work precisely to earn money to get by, and society had informed people as such that when they lose their job, they lose their only viable source of income.

In the working world, a skilled politician revolve around the ability to offer a reversal of this fear and needs on the target- to make job more assured through securing better positions, and as a result having more resources to better the financial situation.

We should not stop at job security, an aspect that is predictably common. In order to have mastery of influence, one should also look into the famous Maslow's hierarchy of needs, a motivational theory in psychology comprising a five-tier model of human needs, often depicted as hierarchical levels. Needs lower down in the hierarchy must be satisfied before individuals can attend to needs higher up. From the bottom of the hierarchy upwards, the needs are: physiological, safety, love and belonging, esteem and self-actualization, within a pyramid. As the names imply, 'Physiological' needs are the most basic, and the 'Self Actualization' needs are most high-minded.

Practically every individual on the planet are deficient of some needs in the Maslow's scheme one way or the other. Even the most successful person with most of the stages fulfilled may be lacking in something. By knowing what a person lacks, one can either help fill the deficiency, or avoid highlighting it offensively. Or knowing what a person holds dear, we can make a show to embrace the preference, and not insult it. And what the person lacks or fears, they usually express with hate.

When one has the ability to identify and address those deep needs in the person's Maslow hierarchy, he or she practically has traversed and appealed to the inner recesses of the person's psyche, making that person subconsciously drawn in and open to influences. Addressing the needs are one thing; potential landmines should also not be triggered.

Example: the boss is a successful career spinster in her 40s who care for animal rights. One can ingratiate oneself to her by claiming same interest in animal rights (appeal to her 'Self Actualization' ideal, reinforcing it), or offend her deeply by talking about how great one's romantic life is (therefore highlighting deficiency in 'Physiological' aspects like sex).

Using Words That Touch the Chord

We are familiar with the idiom, 'Actions Speak Louder Than Words', and universally agree that this is a wise approach. It sets one apart from braggarts, and improves the standing of the person, by putting the substance instead of style at the spotlight. However, let's look at things from another angle. In reality, words actually carry far more potency than action, because they are far more convenient and economical to deploy and offer room for tremendous upsides, than say actual work.

We often see competent workers getting side-lined and underappreciated, while the seemingly less competent staff got all the promotions and increments. The secret of the latter's success tends to have something to do with their ability to use words. When the words touch the chord, words are made flesh. From this, the upsides are exponentially higher, because the right words will both consciously and subconsciously influence the listener. One way to hone this skill is to find out and understand what people really want and then use words that will appeal to them.

John, an IT support staff may be just another guy in his department of 5 other fellow co-workers, perhaps not as well skilled as them when it comes to IT knowledge, but he observed that other teams in the office have complained a lot about passive, slow and unresponsive support from the IT support team. Therefore, he deliberately made points like improved communications and active support at the company's meetings and it is not long before he is promoted to become the IT support team leader.

Lisa is a sales executive in her department of 2 other female sales-person. They are all working equally hard to close deals and hit numbers; and she may not have closed as much deals as her other colleagues. But she always manages to say the right things to Joanne, a closet feminist. She often talks about empowerment for women, women leadership (while the other colleagues are also women, they did not make this connections). Soon enough, when Joanne is promoted to become the sales director, she got Lisa to become the sales manager because she perceives Lisa as sort of 'kindred spirit'.

The thing about the right words is that it connects people because most human beings are impressionable and like to hear good things or things that appeal to their needs and desires or reaffirm their values. On hindsight, be careful of flattery, as this may backfire. Rather, learn to be modest, to appear 'sincere' and subtle when using the words, and be careful of misusing offensive words that may hit home at the listener. As one gets further up the management ladder, it becomes apparent that most of the time, styles and impressions are more pervasive than actual substances because they turn out to be fraternity (or sorority) of vapid ideas, regular bullshits, empty promises, self congratulatory affirmations and insincere reiteration of mission statements.

Subtle Acts of Showing Support

Flattery does not always gets appreciated, especially if the other party can sense the insincerity of this act. I had fun time watching sycophants desperately trying their darndest to please the superiors with just about every of the most obviously contrived and inane tricks in the book of brown-nosing, when I was working in the corporations in the past.

Most attempts were entertained of course, with the superiors playing along and feigning attention and appreciation; but those sycophants always seemed to get played out at the end, forsaken by the same superiors who called their bluffs.

Actually people do like to feel flattered. But flattery almost always doesn't work. You see, the problem lies with the fact that many of these bootlickings are done too blatantly obvious. When one performs such acts conspicuously and unpracticed enough without finesse, it illicit the impression of being told lies about one's capability, and being felt like getting made use of, or taken for a fool to further the success of the other party; it also tends to attract the attention from other office colleagues who will cringe and feel disgusted after witnessing such desperate attempts.

But if a person can manage to get the other party flattered, without using flattery, he or she might be able to inch closer to winning the heart of the target. In order to get there, one should consider how to perform subtle acts of showing support to the intended targets.

One may begin by using subtle compliments. Let's say that Boris, the operations director came up with a materials sourcing proposal. Given his seniority, and possibility of succession plans, many of his subordinates tried to fawn over him by praising his work.

Boris had seen enough of these types; those wretches with brown noses and smiles of sick desperation. However, he was rather flattered when he came across a powerpoint presentation slide with parts citing his proposal, without prior knowledge. After he asked around, he found out that the slide deck belonged to Joseph, the purchasing manager, and somehow this minor gesture played a part in influencing the latter's promotion subsequently.

From the above, we can see that the compliments, praises or support were not issued directly, but rather slipped in through a medium. Rather than been informed of them, Boris came to find out this information by himself.

This can play out in other manner- a person talking to intended target, but slipped elements of support through an unrelated topic, which the target figured out himself later on. The key factors therefore, are: being **indirect**, using a **medium or unrelated topic** to carry or mask the message, and structure them in a way whereby there is a high probability that the **target will personally find out or realize.**

Meeting the Bosses of the Boss

Throughout the book, you'd have noticed that I frequently mentioned about the importance of getting attention, and even audience from the Bosses of the Boss, and beyond. However, it may be difficult because:

a) The Bosses of the Boss (or beyond), given their seniority, may be distant from the employee, and therefore out of reach.

b) The Boss will not like it if you are seen talking to anyone more senior than the Boss, especially his or her own Boss.

c) The act is disobeying the Chain-of-Command (covered under "Know the Hierarchy") which have severe consequences.

Besides attempting to catch this person when the immediate boss is not around, there is a legit but risky route which I've personally attempted and succeeded. That is, to leverage help, from the Human Resources.

When I was a junior staff suffering under the leadership of a fatuous boss, I had several innovative ideas which could help the team, but were largely ignored or put down by that person. This action from the immediate supervisor became an impediment to the progress of both the team, as well as to myself. I decided to seek help from the Human Resources department, and managed to even speak to the Head of the HR. The Head of the HR contacted the Boss of the Boss, and I was therefore given an audience with this person, without my immediate boss's knowledge. Needless to say, the Boss of the Boss liked my ideas and gave me the permission to execute them. By then, he also formed a rather negative impression of my immediate boss. In no time, I became the head of the team, and the old fatuous boss was side-lined.

The above act may be risky as it can incur the wrath of the immediate boss (this will be found out sooner or later), but there are certain merits:

a) It does not break the Chain-of-Command because I did not seek out the Boss of the Boss myself; I was assisted by the help of the HR department, which had this person initiating a private meeting for me.

b) If there are genuinely good ideas which can contribute to the success of the team or the organization, the Boss of the Boss will be all ears, because successes will also amplify his or her image as the overall leader.

c) If the Boss of the Boss is at your side, you've earned yourself a potentially strong political backer, especially if you already planned to overtake the authority of your Boss.

All the above been said, only use this strategy when you are sufficiently prepared, with ideas that have high chances of contributing to successes.

Dealing with
Problematic Subordinates

When I was in middle management, I was sandwiched between having to meet the expectations of my superiors, and also having to get the subordinates to be cooperative and perform their tasks. I ran my team well, with many supportive subordinates, but there were always one or two difficult subordinates who gave me problems; not just work problems, but attitude problems and general disrespect. Regardless of whether a person is a good leader, there are always bound to be some black sheep in existence.

I had seen how the other leaders tried all sorts of methods; ranging from gentle persuasions (and then the subordinates eventually went over their heads), and fiery vitriolic (and then the subordinates made a beeline to the HR to lodge complaints) and failed miserably, exhausted and exasperated by the problematic subordinates. To be effective in dealing with problematic subordinates, one should not get emotional, or compromising, but to employ psychological threats which will strike deeper into the recesses of their souls.

One method which always proved effective for me is to: delegate crucial, key and difficult task to the subordinates; to set them up for failure. I had this problematic saleswoman who thought she was better than everyone else and even doubted my capability. She did not deliver results or hit her targets, but would often complain about being treated unfairly, how she was given lousy accounts to handle and would frequently go around complaining, smearing the reputation of the team.

I decided that I did not want to keep her, but realized that there were no solid grounds to fire her. So, I gave her a task: to handle one of the largest, and most difficult key account. I told her that since she always complained that there were no solid accounts to handle, this was one of the best opportunities to shine. She tendered her resignation the next day.

There is always a 20% chance that this person will accept and stay on, but given the lack of competency, this person will still end up in failure, giving more valid grounds for dismissal.

Identify and Exploit
Conflict Points

Conflict Points are first discussed in "Find Out the Political Factions" under the chapter "Knowledge and Propriety". In the same topic, I mentioned that 'Cues' are more literal observations of two parties: how they interact, any perceived hostility and discontent, and if they have even openly admitted their dislikes for the other party during those pantry sessions. 'Conflict Points' are the tensions based on rational analysis on philosophical and competitive differences.

The reason why we need to identify and exploit conflict points is because it is more deep seated and potent, than the visual cues. 'Cues' can sometimes be misleading, but 'Conflict Points' are usually definitive.

As part of a political strategy, it is useful to take note of any potential conflict points which can arise from interaction of your enemy targets (could be anyone from your overbearing boss, to your competitive colleague) and act on them to score political points. These people, or almost anybody, who have worked for a while, is bound to encounter tensions with someone else or groups, due to differences and disagreements with work. I have mentioned before that 'Givers/Recipients' relationships across the different departments and job functions, as well as the overarching philosophical forces between 'Status Quo' and 'New Order' tend to be fertile grounds for conflict.

The keys to exploiting these conflict points are to **remediate**, **insinuate** and **aggravate**. Remediate is possibly the safest. Sometimes, other tactics like insinuate and aggravate can also be used, only requiring a certain level of finesse and risk taking to pull off successfully. These tactics do not have to follow any order. Read carefully on what they entail.

Remediate- provides a remedy for; redress or make right. If we use your rival colleague as an example, he might have incurred dissatisfaction from other colleagues over certain work not properly done. Are you able to therefore, bridge the gap where it lacked, to bring value to the other colleagues, thus undermining the capability of the rival colleague further, while fostering better relationship between them and yourself?

Remediation is one of the oldest trick in the books of politics and mankind. It is best exemplified in Hegelian Dialectic: a thesis, giving rise to its reaction; an antithesis, which contradicts or negates the thesis; and the tension between the two being resolved by means of a solution. These has happened in almost all parts of human history and conflicts.

Remediation is thus, the solution in the dialectic, and it is valued rather highly in view of the management, because if one is capable of resolving some problems, he or she may thus be able solve other other problems in the company.

Insinuate- suggest or hint (something bad) in an indirect and unpleasant way. Are you able to bring to knowledge to someone important, or of sufficient power about how the rival colleague is not doing the work properly, as an existing problem which affects the overall function? Such hints should be subtle, and preferably should not come from yourself, but have a junior office gossip to do the work they are best at: dispensing information company wide.

Aggravate- make (a problem, injury, or offence) worse or more serious. Make the problem seems larger than ever before. Blow up the matter by cautiously using tactics such as garnering external bad feedback from customers to highlight to the management (remember, never directly present any of these, but use other conveyors or medium to get message across, to the senior management), which is usually more damaging than internal complaints from other colleagues about the certain work not properly done. At the same time, amplify and broadcast how your remediation is helping to address the existing problem, also to the senior management.

Remediation, Insinuation and Aggravation also do not need to be directed at one party all the same time. Sometimes it is possible to remediate for one party, and insinuate or aggravate at the other party. There is a possibility of deflections, reversions and even redirecting conflicts to different sides. But they may sometimes backfire more dangerously, and it should only be applied to the nastiest rivals.

Do Not Correct Egoistical Rivals

Your competitors or even your own boss may disagree with the way you do things, and insist on their way or the highway. Many of the readers are no strangers to this scenario, and often time, would have wasted time and energy trying to convince, persuade, correct and beg to differ; getting exasperated and exhausted with obstinate and conceited, self righteous colleagues.

If they have a likelihood with being wrong, do not step in to correct them or assist them, especially if they are considered rivals by your definition, but rather do allow them to continue to be wrong, down the path of perdition by their own doing, which will hopefully lead to their demise in the organization.

By not interfering with them, you also would have made them consider you as less of a threat (for people with dominant personality who always insist on getting what they want, they tend to be egoistical and a bit stupid when it comes to subtlety and covert motives), and relax their guards around you. They may even be convinced that their ideas or plans are superior, thus reaffirming their self beliefs as genius.

Let these people keep repeating those mistakes, and they will eventually contribute to their own personal downfall.

Tune In to Rivals

You have identified your enemies, competitors, detractors and haters. Let's refer them collectively as the "Rivals". You may be carrying out your political plans, but they could also be doing the same- nothing stopping them from actively planning your downfall. But they will behave friendly and smile at you, because you always do the same to them, although you know very well that they couldn't wait to tear you apart.

Such is the reality of politics in the working world; it really involves more mind games than physical forces, but the damages done could also be much more profound and extensive. The damages tend not to be sporadic, but chronic, insidious and long term. Wouldn't it be great if you can know what they are up to, so you can prepare to fend and stop them before they happen? As the saying goes, "Keep your friends close, and your enemies closer (Sun Tzu, Petrach, The Godfather)". This quote can mean a lot of things- know your enemies well, pay closer attention to our enemies than friends, or even turn your enemies into your friends.

I have different opinions about this quote. I believe friends are more dangerous than enemies, because enemies are obvious and friends are not. Friends can turn into the most dangerous 'hidden' enemies, who can harm you in the most unexpected way. If I have to update the quote, I have this interpretation:

keep friends at a distance so they won't turn into your enemies (often, so called friendships are destroyed when the friends get too close together, because intimacy tends to bring out more flaws and differences between individuals); keep enemies close by so you can tune in to threats, and potentially convert them to friendly forces. To be tuned in to the rivals, one does not necessarily have to get close to them. It is possible to do it through third parties. During encounters or meetings, do read between the lines to sense where the person is heading and anticipate threats if any. See if it is even possible to find out what conflict points the person have with you, so you can readily choose to act on them.

A skilled politician can sometimes even turn the enemy into a political ally if there is a meeting of needs. Assuming there is already a rift caused by a conflict point, it is still possible to remediate this conflict point by mending relations between the two parties, and insinuate/aggravate these issues to a third party, to 'redirect' blame and conflict to the other targets. Some may argue that this practice is immoral, but this lesser act of evil can bring down the knees of the greater evil.

Let's use a simple example: Margaret (technical editor, a rival) is unhappy with Jason (copywriter) for lack of quality in the content (and see him as rival for her position). Jason may act to remediate this conflict by submitting to Margaret with improved quality work and agreement with her, while (redirect) insinuating that another party (the sales team-nastier rivals) have been securing poor leads from technology companies, thereby (redirect) aggravations between Margaret and sales team, and bringing Margaret to his side.

The Power of Escalations

Things could have progressed in a very ugly manner, where the veneer of civility is wearing thin, and rancor is emerging. It may be a decisive battle which determines your fate in the company, in the face of oppositions. Opponents may force you into a position with only two choices- fight or flight. At this point keep the cool head and think hard- what are the other options you can likely take?

Let's go back to school days and recall the backyard fights between the boys. Weaker boys who were pummeled by the stronger bullies, not just once, but several times throughout the school terms, always got drawn into the backyard to face the challenge. The weaker boys saw only two options- fight the bullies or try to run away, but either options are catch 22- they will lose their creds losing to the bullies, but will even stand to lose more and get called sissies, if they run away like cowards.

However, there was always that one boy who would never have to put up with this sort of nonsense. In terms of physical constitution, he was not any better than the weaker boys; indeed he was a scrawny little guy. But he was a clever one. Bullies tend to stay away from him to stay out of trouble. Because if bullies were to taunt him, he would made a beeline to the headmaster, and always got the boys punished.

Going back to the office, if one get into a fight or flight scenario, do not give in to any of them, but do what the smart boy did- **escalate** the matter. How does this exactly work?

After having gotten far into the political positioning, a person should be able to anticipate the threats and the danger (opportunities) moments that come along. When an antagonistic party comes down at your throat; hijacking and disrupting your work, or tarnishing your name, getting you into a losing possibility or stalemate, escalations may often prove to be handy. There are many ways escalations can be played.

To escalate, means to make or become more serious or intense. It is different from 'aggravate' in conflict points. Escalate brings things to a higher level (i.e. to the superior, or authority), than make things messier in 'aggravate'. Let's look at what are the different possible escalations:

1.) **The Work Disruption Escalation**- To call out that one's work has been compromised by disruption of one party. When work function is hijacked, especially important or high revenue churning works or projects, it brings valid concerns for the management to do something about it, because it is all in the SOP, and they are obliged to do something about it to evince their professional duties.

2.) **The Harassment Escalation**- When the opponents bother an employee a lot, especially when there are documentable abuses, it is valid ground to play the harassment card. Usually this has to be coupled with both the management and human resources (especially in MNCs), because HR, one of the weakest department in the company is also potentially one of the most powerful. Most HR decisions are either in accordance or overridden by the senior management, but when it comes to harassments, especially along the line of very controversial subjects like race, religion, gender- the harassment card played at the human resources department can turn into the most powerful weapon against the opponents, because they will do whatever they can to protect their diversity embracing image, and the opponents can get into potentially very serious trouble. This is one of the most potent card to use.

3.) **The Conflict Point Escalation**- Remember we used to look at how to identify and exploit using conflict points? Now put it to good use to escalate to the relevant party, and serve out the cold dishes (remediate, insinuate, escalate) accordingly, to undermine the character or capability of the opponent.

4.) **The Conspicuous Escalation**- This is where you do not go on the offensive against your opponents, but rather choose to unleash your hidden cards to impress all those who matters. This is where "Time Your Performance", "Raise Visibility Carefully" and "The Kairotic Moment" come into play, showing and upselling yourself to the Top Dogs your capability, ability, skill sets, and bedazzle them so much that they will root for you than your rivals.

Graduation of Power

Some readers may perhaps disagree with my constant advocating of 'modesty', because of its slightly self-deprecatory connotations. There are many self-improvement books and videos out there strongly advocating the total opposite of my approach, extolling the need for strong and powerful self-image. I would implore the readers to ponder the utility of my approach.

When an employee first starts out in any job or company, especially at a junior position; having displays of power are not rational. Because there will be no advantage in looking better and more powerful than the boss and other co-workers. A junior worker is expected to be transigent to the boss, and if the person behaves cocky, it tends to illicit dislikes, and end up getting seen as having a big head, an object of ridicule.

There is no problem with looking confident, and handling the work relatively well; the only problem is not to appear too strong to transgress the rules within "Hide Your Shine".

When the employee becomes more well adjusted and advances to a higher position, displays of overwhelming strength and power brings about another set of thoughts: envy, insecurity and competition, to both the bosses and co-workers alike. There should be a gradual projection of power since the transition from a junior worker; the ability to appear more competent, and having the confidence to act decisively. But the employee needs to keep this slight power in check, never to look like one is blatantly trying to out compete the boss and co-workers.

At a senior position, especially between middle to upper management, the employee may need to bring up the display of power several notches. Exceptional strengths and confidence should exude from this person, because he or she is expected to be the leader of teams and departments, and an authority to be reckoned with, especially to the subordinates. He or she should appear strong and powerful enough to make sure the subordinates toe the line and obediently perform the tasks well.

Despite all the displays of power, the person at the senior management should still be mindful not to transgress upwards to the Top Dogs.

At the peak, with great power comes great responsibility, as corny as it sounds. This power should helm the company through challenging courses and bring it to greater heights. This power should influence and inspire the employees to grow with the company. This power should keep the power of other senior executives in check and make them subservient to its prowess. This power should be felt but not fathomed.

Because true power should not be easily discerned, otherwise it is not true power.

When Political Endeavor Fails

Politics is always risky business, and if one wagers for victories, one should also get prepared for failures. Despite all the efforts that were made, when it comes to this point, it probably means that you should revisit other options.

Usually things may not turn out as bad as one expected; frequently, the loser can get away by shutting up and getting on with work. But there are also instances whereby losing will put one in a very disadvantageous position, especially when the rival winners start their hot pursuit go decimate fallen rivals. When that happens, keep calm and move on.

Earlier in the book, under "The Daily Grind", I had discussed the need to "Always Have Contingency". Having a backup plan always serve to help anyone in the most unfavorable of outcome. There are also several strategies one can choose to take, should things don't turn out in one's favor.

Retreat- At this point, the employee can either remove oneself from the political arena, or stop the political pursuit, resetting the neutral button. Failures are part and parcel of life, and with some battles lost, it does not necessarily mean that the war is lost. Resume low profile and cease political activities, while actively keep an active lookout for opportunities, both inside and outside the company, recuperate and plan out the next moves in silence.

Remediate- If one falls out with the winners, there may still be some rooms (conflict points) left for remediation. It is sometimes possible to iron out the differences, calls truce, or even submit oneself to the winning factions. This can probably make the employee feel more miserable, having to now bear the shame of surrender and submission to the enemies, but a seasoned politician will see this as a necessary move to ensure survival, and to even get closer to the enemies. When the time is right, there is no stopping a coup from happening.

Escape- Perhaps one had also been on the lookout for potential job opportunities outside this wretched company? When there are no more hopes left within the organization, it is always at the best interest of the person to leave the company to embark on new career endeavor.

Escape may be involuntary (getting retrenched) or voluntary (quitting the job). If one chooses to quit, it is advisable to always quit at the peak of the career (when there are several achievements to show), because it will raise credence and value to the next potential employers. If one is unfortunate to be a victim of the political struggle, getting booted out by the company in the process; just accept this fact, take a break, and move on to greener pastures (you will be ensured a higher chance of success in getting the next job if you've always been constantly on the look out).

Fortune Favors the Patient

"Oh Fortune, like the moon, you are changeable, ever waxing and waning.." The ebb and flow of fortune are ephemeral, and when luck runs out and hits the bottom, where do you go next? Things will usually look up. If only most people comprehend that such is the celestial mechanisms of fate.

In order for one to get successful again, after periods of failures, the only way is to ride the tide and wait out. Patience is a virtue, and a utility. It requires certain fortitude, situational awareness and faith. Imagine this in financial analogy: a trader who compulsively sells his position in the stock will realize actual physical losses. If he or she does nothing, the losses are only on paper. And if the positions are held longer, the losses may one day turn into profits when situation improves.

Assuming the employee has failed in his or her goals in the company, there is no need to deem it the end of the world; there are always opportunities in the future to make a comeback, well recuperated and resurging enthusiasm.

Keep calm and stay patient when bad outcome happens, lady luck will return to your side again.

Afterword

The reader might have noted that the chapters are set in different phases of a corporate job cycle of a "relatively ambitious employee", beginning with significantly longer periods of dormancy (preparation and fortification), and punctuated by short and swift decisive actions when appropriate. This cycle, may or may not be pertinent to different career situations of the readers.

The individual entries, on the other hand, are by and large relating to commonplace situations at work which most will find applicable. One of course need not diligently follow all the suggestions here, but it is of best interest to know them and add to expanding one's insights and perspectives. Many of the strategies are heuristically derived from the more effective case studies; which turn out frequently contrarian, as many readers would have noted.

Of imperative note is the key message of the book: be adaptable. When situations deem fit, prepare to perform reversals of the strategies, to break some rules when necessary, and always be ready to embrace the constancy of change. With the expanded insights and perspectives, coupled with honed instincts and intelligence, they will surely see the employee through far and wide- to survive and thrive.

.

ABOUT THE AUTHOR

Rick Lazarus had previously written several critically acclaimed books under a different name. This book is the first in the series of instructive guides offering novel, and contrarian insights and secret strategies to enable the readers to survive and thrive in any situations. His life mission is to empower the disenfranchised. He enjoys doing all of the above in privacy and reclusion.

Website: https://ricklazarus.com